Dear Friend,

For over six years I've felt all kinds of feelings at Dimes, whether in my own head or together with friends. At Dimes I've cried — if you're a New Yorker at some point you've cried in public — but I've also tried, lied, appetized, been baptized, sighed, realized, eyed, felt fried, and sometimes, felt larger-than-life-sized. Before Dimes, I used to experience my feelings in private in my tiny Chinatown apartment on Division Street. Then Dimes opened downstairs and finally — tears of joy — I could get a decent morning coffee in the neighborhood; a good glass of wine at night. Dimes became an extension of my apartment, as a perfect place to commiserate or celebrate, but also an extension of my kitchen. Subtly, over years, Dimes became an extension of my life-appetite too: A place to digest New York City life. A state of hunger for unknown pleasures. A place to eat up crazy people, cooking up wild ideas and igniting even-crazier desires. Dimes became a place to satisfy the stomach and life-appetite with Emotional Eating.

As Dimes grew in the neighborhood, birthing a deli and market, I would crane my head out of my apartment window to see how crowded the restaurant was across the street and gauge if there was anyone downstairs at the deli so I could get a quick bite in, and feel surrounded by people. I would usually spot either Alissa or Sabrina, the two plucky women behind Dimes, zipping between the two locations, arms loaded, exchanging quick words with quick steps, spreading hellos and smiles to all the folks along the way, leaving invisible trails in their wake.

The mark of a truly great neighborhood restaurant — part of being open every day of the week — is to a have a generosity of spirit, found not only in comforting food, but in being a respite of sorts, a place generous enough to absorb the most unruly emotions of its regulars, of which I am one. Regulars perfecting the lively art of running into each other in the neighborhood, living out lives on Canal Street.

Like many others in the neighborhood, I developed a regular order — coffee with whole milk, the daily juice, breakfast tacos with bacon, salsa on the side — dropping in at regular times of the day, and then days of the week (never on a Saturday), finding peace in pink salmon, orange wine, and black rice, and refuge in Dimes's steady rhythms, helping to navigate the emo-moodiness contained in a New York minute. I grew fond of eavesdropping on awkward first dates and curing homesickness with pozole, the familiar scene playing out like a favorite movie, with an ever-expanding cast of characters each with their distinct vibe, usual order, and specific style of Emotional Eating.

There is a musicality to Dimes in its daily routines:

Put the glasses on the table. Chop through a mountain of onions without shedding a tear. The wait this morning is Oh about 35 minutes (truly an hour...) A breakup conversation at the table next to you. Tears. Check please. A first date conversation at the table on the left. Nerves. Order to share. You'll bring your parents from Oklahoma to Dimes and introduce them to green juice. Your parents will definitely not like it, but they eventually might — that's the hope. There will always be new "freak-abana" flowers each week. The flowers will die. Yes. Yes of course you can add an avocado on that. No. No, don't yell at me; can't you see I'm busy? Dimes Market will always have some sage to burn, some eggs to crack.

Emotional Eating is a kind of hopeful yearning, a hunger to be with people even on days you can barely get out of bed or barely think straight. When it's comforting to get your usual at Dimes if only to utter your first words of the day, even at 1:29 in the afternoon. This book is an invitation to share the Dimes Times vibe with you, wherever you are so you're not so alone.

Life is almost never a perfect ten, but we can try together at Dimes.

Love,
X

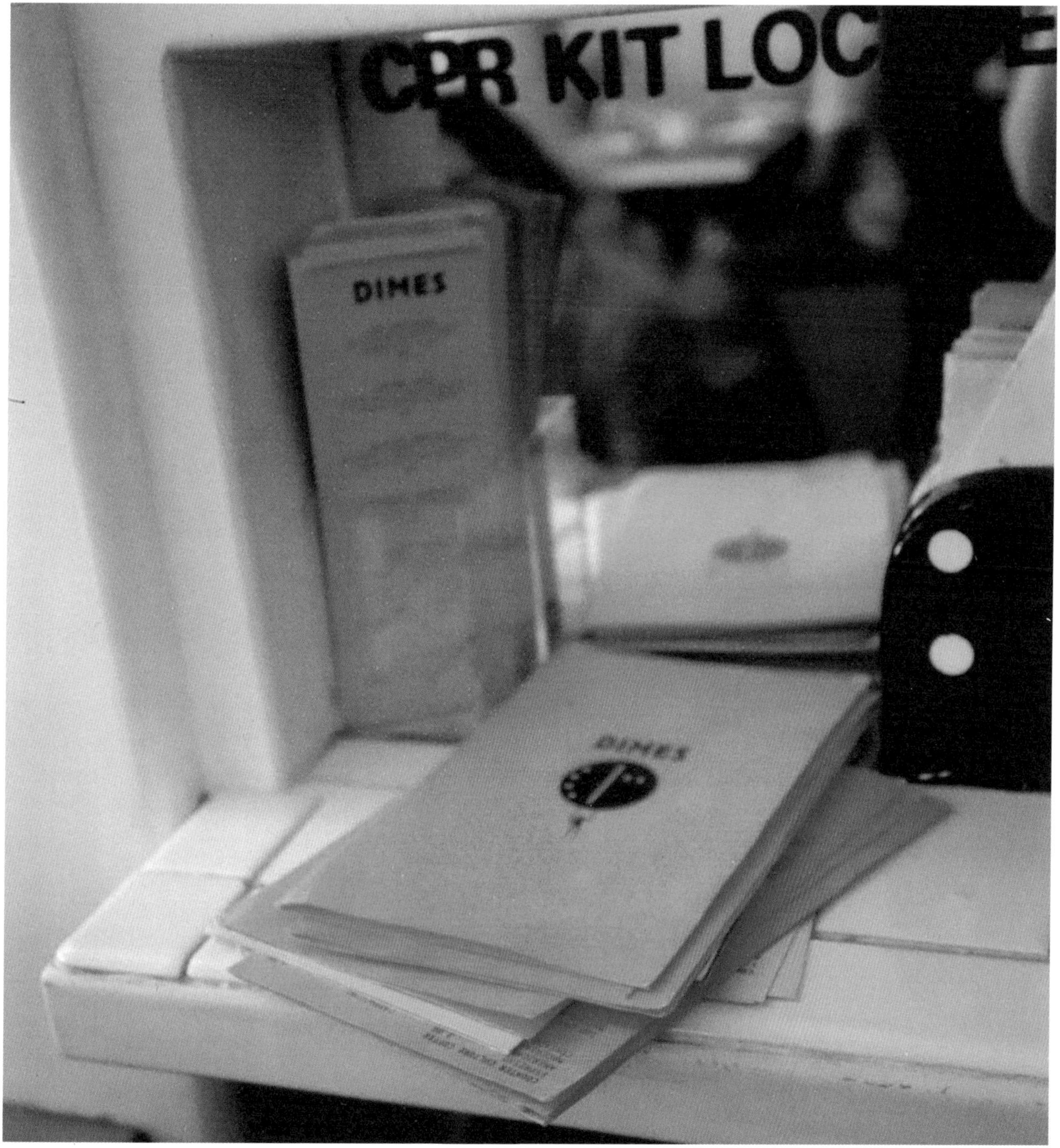
CPR KIT LOC
DIMES
DIMES

DIMES TIMES

EMOTIONAL EATING

| 4:20 PM | FOUR TWENTY | 98 |

| 6:00 PM | HOMESICK | 100 |

Cornbread	104
Dimes Chili	105
Curry	106
Alberto's Pozole	107
Moqueca — Brazilian Fish Stew	108
Shepherd's Pie	109
Vegan Mac + Cheese	110
Winter Veg + White Bean Casserole	111

| 8:00 PM | HONEYMOON | 112 |

Broiled Sardines	117
Shrimp + Fonio Grits	118
Harissa Roasted Cod	120
Baked Sole	121
Poaching Liquid	122
Homemade Furikake	125

| 10:00 PM | COMMISERATE | 126 |

Wheatgrass Margarita	131
Milk River	131
Loving Love	131
Ume Shiso Seltzer	133
Guava-Tahini Colada	133
PH Tonic	133
Flourless Chocolate cake	135

| 11:00 PM | AFTERHOURS | 136 |

BLOOD ORANGE
A juicy, fiery sunset packed
with vitamin C and cancer-
fighting anthocyanins.
page 46, 62, 63, 83, 120

ALMOND
Cute. Small. Easy to Eat.
Alkalizing. A pocket-sized
snack to keep you balanced.
page 26 (milk), 27, 29, 65,
90, 111

BANANA
Full of minerals. Tons of
vitamin C. Comes with
its own carrying case. Yellow.
page 24, 26, 27, 30, 135

BEANS
Beans, beans, the musical...
sorry. High in minerals
including iron and zinc and
packed with protein, beans
are a powerful dietary staple.

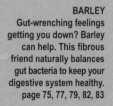

BARLEY
Gut-wrenching feelings
getting you down? Barley
can help. This fibrous
friend naturally balances
gut bacteria to keep your
digestive system healthy.

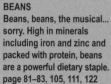

AVOCADO
AvocaDONT ignore me.
My healthy fats help
YOU absorb nutrients from
other vegetables. I also have
tons of my own nutrients
which I'd love to share with
you. P.S. I won't break
your heart, I'll nourish it.

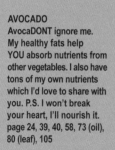

CELERY
Keeps the pee coming and
your blood squeaky clean.

GINGER

No, no of course you're not hungover. Food poisoning, totally. Well, in any event, you're still nauseous. Why not have some ginger to settle your stomach and improve your circulation to boot?

GARLIC

Eliminates toxins. Antibacterial, antifungal, anti-Vampire.

MUSHROOM

One side makes you grow taller, the other side, shorter. Some are magic. All are detoxifiers.

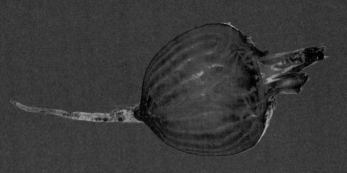

BEET

Surfing the crimson wave? Haul ass to a beet smoothie. Beets help with PMS-related sads and mads and are a natural blood tonic.

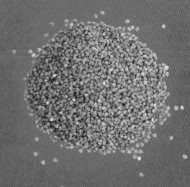

FLAX
Don't let them see you sweat. Fiber-rich flax seed regulates and softens bowel movements. Spend more time doing things you love.
page 25, 27, 46, 62, 63, 65

BUCKWHEAT
"I can't eat gluten," —Everyone, 2019. Buckwheat is your new grocery crush. Gluten free and packed with B-complex vitamins for increased energy levels, brain function, and metabolism.
page 54, 55, 135

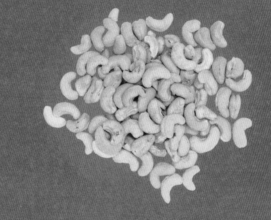

CASHEW
"CaSHEW!" "Gesundheit." If you've got the shivers from a nasty cold, cashews' warming and immunity-boosting properties will help you back to health.
page 27, 29, 65, 78, 82, 90, 95

APPLE CIDER VINEGAR
We're all different but we all have a mother. Unlike most, THIS mother aids circulation, cleanses, and battles fatigue.
page 55, 63, 91, 94–96, 111, 117, 133

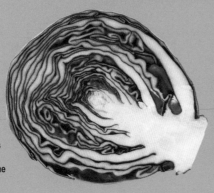

CABBAGE
Often straight to video,
cabbage is low in calories
and high in nutrition,
especially rich in antioxidants
and vitamin K. Use extra
large leaves for your own Anne
Geddes-inspired photoshoot.
page 65, 83, 96, 125

TOMATILLO
This pre-Columbian
nightshade and Mexican
staple supports ocular
health and fights cancer.
page 39, 107

MANGO
Cutting around the formidable
oblong mango pit can be a
deterrent to the faint of heart.
Persist and be rewarded
with the juicy, heat-clearing
fruit rich in vitamins A and C.
page 25, 27, 39, 91, 93

CARROTS
Carrots keep your eyes
sharp with beta carotene-
sourced vitamin A. Makes
a classic snowman nose.
page 25, 65, 73, 82, 83, 92,
94, 96, 109, 125

DATES
If you're like most of us,
your liver is probably more
GWAR than Gwyneth.
Have a date. Have several.
page 24, 28

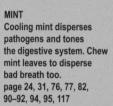

MINT
Cooling mint disperses
pathogens and tones
the digestive system. Chew
mint leaves to disperse
bad breath too.
page 24, 31, 76, 77, 82,
90–92, 94, 95, 117

FISH
Stay sharp, rest up, and be
happy. Eating fish helps
lower the risk of alzheimer's,
improves sleep quality,
and reduces symptoms
of depression.
pages 46, 75, 108, 116–125

FIG
A great name for a dog (you're welcome), this gorgeous fruit increases energy and is high in depression-fighting magnesium.

CHICKPEAS
A lover not a fighter, the chickpea supports the heart, controls the appetite, and benefits digestion.

COCONUT MILK
Increases semen, tonifies the heart, tastes like coconut. Need we say more?

CILANTRO
Too much Iron Maiden on your playlist? Cilantro helps rid the body of heavy metals while its natural sedative properties reduce anxiety.

EGGS
Inside this fragile shell
lives a nutrient powerhouse
packed with high quality
proteins and omega-3s.
Great for vandalism.
page 36–41, 135

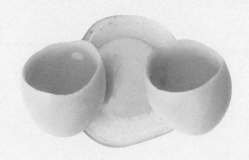

FENNEL
This favorite stimulates
lactation and treats
indigestion. Which you
will surely have if
you are a new mom.
page 24, 40 (seeds), 46,
55 (seeds), 62, 63, 65, 76
(seeds), 78 (seeds), 80
(seeds), 82, 83, 94 (seeds),
96, 109, 120, 122 (seeds),
123 (seeds), 131 (seeds)

SAGE
Eat fresh sage to exorcise
mucus and relax muscles.
Burn dried sage to exorcise
bad spirits and relax
the atmosphere.
page 58, 59, 79, 80,
109–111, 125

LEMON
A kitchen flavor giant,
this sunny fruit aids
digestion, helps you pee, and
supports liver function.
page 30, 55, 74, 76–79, 83,
90, 92, 94, 95, 111, 117,
120–122, 131, 133

THAI CHILI
Embrace the heat. The
capsaicin in chilis
delivers a wide variety
of anti-inflammatory,
immunity-boosting, and
tonifying benefits.
page 37, 40, 91, 107

KALE
"Hey, yoo hoo, it's me,
Kale. I'm still here. I'm still
number 1. I'm never gonna
stop. I'm basically Beyonce."
High in chlorophyll, calcium,
and iron this endlessly
talented superfood is here
to stay.
page 24, 37, 46, 63, 65, 71, 76,
79, 83, 90, 105, 108, 111

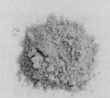

MATCHA
Naughty by nature?
Matcha detoxifies while
calming the mind
and relaxing the body.
page 36

SESAME
This tiny seed is the David
to nuts' Goliath, containing
more protein than any
nut around.
page 29, 37, 41, 65, 78,
104, 124, 125

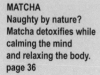

KIMCHI
Anti-aging and immune-
boosting — we need
all the help we can get.
page 41, 80 (paste)

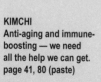

GOCHUJANG
This culinary secret weapon
spices things up while
boosting metabolism and
supporting a healthy heart.
page 37, 41, 80

TURMERIC
Will stain your fingers and clothes but you won't be mad at it because the color is so pretty and you will be so anti-inflamed, anti-oxidized, and devoid of free radicals.
page 80, 83, 94–97, 118, 119, 131

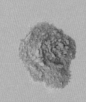

WILD RICE
This aquatic grass is rich in proteins, minerals and B vitamins that promote a healthy pregnancy and help to reduce birth defects.
page 75, 76

RICE VINEGAR
I might be poor on paper but I'm rich in amino acids.
page 37, 41, 51, 91, 110

SWEET POTATO
High in vitamin A, C, and carotenoid antioxidants. Tell your kids it's potato candy to get them to eat vegetables.
page 30, 65, 71, 73, 83, 111

FREEKEH
This champion grain
contains gut-healing
prebiotics and glutamic
acid which synthesizes
glutamine to build
endurance and strength.
A must for athletes.
page 75, 76, 125

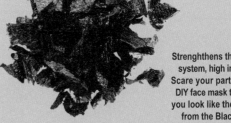

NORI
Strenghthens the immune
system, high in minerals.
Scare your partner with a
DIY face mask that makes
you look like the Creature
from the Black Lagoon.
page 37, 125

MISO
Miso may be beige in color
but its personality is anything
but. This unassuming powerhouse is an anticarcinogen
and is effective in reducing
the effects of radiation,
smoking, air pollution and
other environmental toxins.
page 79, 80, 83, 95, 104, 111,
118, 119, 125

YOGURT
Nutrient dense,
high in protein, relieves
itchy hoo-has.
page 28, 54, 95, 105, 120

8:00 AM

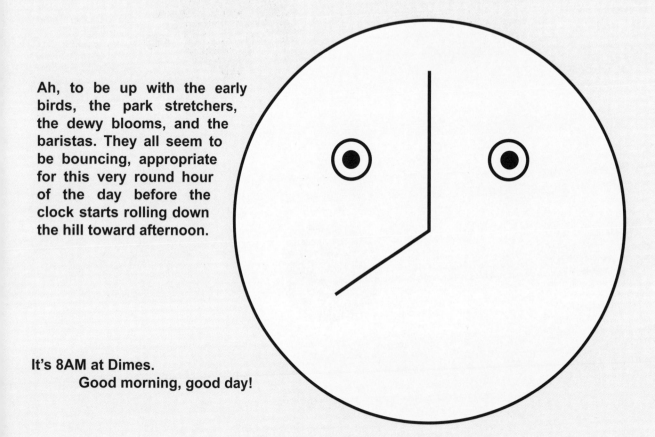

Ah, to be up with the early birds, the park stretchers, the dewy blooms, and the baristas. They all seem to be bouncing, appropriate for this very round hour of the day before the clock starts rolling down the hill toward afternoon.

It's 8AM at Dimes.
Good morning, good day!

Face in the sun,

Hello, face of the sun!
Hello, flowers,

what a marvelous allium!

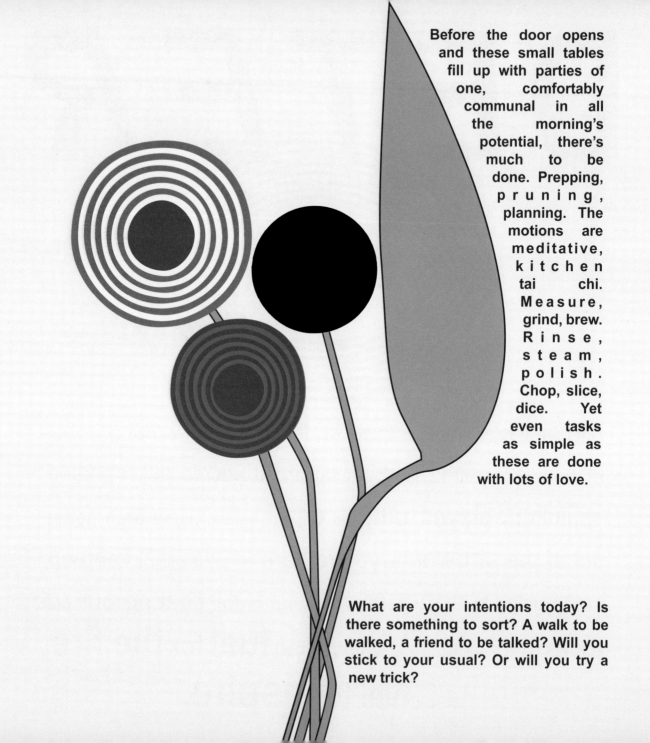

Before the door opens and these small tables fill up with parties of one, comfortably communal in all the morning's potential, there's much to be done. Prepping, pruning, planning. The motions are meditative, kitchen tai chi. Measure, grind, brew. Rinse, steam, polish. Chop, slice, dice. Yet even tasks as simple as these are done with lots of love.

What are your intentions today? Is there something to sort? A walk to be walked, a friend to be talked? Will you stick to your usual? Or will you try a new trick?

DETERM

It's fast here. **Faster** than where you're from, **faster** than you're used to. It can seem like ideas are given birth to, developed, romanced, adored, **appropriated,** **exploited, played out,** and **dead** before you've even gotten out of the **shower.** But **you're here** — you're going to **keep up,** you're going to **conquer.** This hour is for **figuring out** what **tricks to try,** and whatever you decide, **you'll need fuel for the fire.** You need **fuel to inspire.**

These recipes will help you begin your day with a jump start. Powerful antioxidants and immune-boosting, health-supportive ingredients will keep you in fighting shape so you can charge through life with purpose and determination. Go on, get out there, you tenacious thing, you!

SM●◉THIES

Smoothies can be a true lifeline in terms of getting a lot of raw
nutrients in your body really quickly and easily. A common
thread among New Yorkers is near constant next-level hustling.
If you're like us, it's not uncommon for a whole day
to go by before you realized you haven't had time to eat.
Smoothies are perfect for those busy on-your-feet days
because they are completely portable nutritional powerhouses.
They're like CliffsNotes for a healthy diet.

WHITE

1   frozen banana   ½ cup coconut milk
¼ cup diced fennel   ½ tsp vanilla extract
½ tsp coconut flakes   1-2 ice cubes
1   tsp rice bran

GREEN

4-5 frozen   1   tbsp lime juice
    pineapple chunks   ½ inch piece peeled
½ cup kale,   fresh ginger root
    loosely packed   ½ cup coconut water
1   pitted date   ½ an avocado
3   mint leaves   1-2 ice cubes

UPGRADES AND THEIR BENEFITS

Follow guidelines on the package for how much to add.

FLAX SEED — omega-3s / improve cholesterol / high quality protein

MACA — increases fertility / improves mood / reduces sun damage / fights free radicals

SPIRULINA — antioxidant / anti-cancer properties

MORINGA — antioxidant / reduces inflammation / lowers blood sugar levels

REISHI — immune-boosting / supports physical and mental well-being

ASHWAGANDHA — reduces stress and anxiety / decreases cortisol levels

ACTIVATED CHARCOAL — removes toxins / anti-aging properties

ORANGE

1 cup diced carrot
5 mango chunks
5 papaya chunks
2 basil leaves
½ tsp camu camu

½ cup freshly squeezed orange juice
1-2 ice cubes

Place all ingredients in the pitcher of a blender. Blend for about 2 minutes or until very smooth. Makes 12oz.

BERRY ACAI

SERVES 1

1 packet acai (100g) broken into pieces
½ frozen banana
3 frozen strawberries
3 frozen raspberries
1 cup almond milk, plus more for desired consistency if necessary

¼ cup goji granola (p 29)
½ cup mixed fresh sliced strawberries, raspberries, and blueberries.

Using the tamper continually, blend in a blender for about 2 to 3 minutes until completely smooth and creamy. It should be thick enough to eat with a spoon. Add more almond milk as necessary to achieve desired consistency.

MAKE IT YOURS

Use any other mix of frozen fruit in place of, or
in addition to those listed in the recipe. Swap out the
almond milk for coconut milk, hemp milk, or oat milk.
You can even use water in a pinch. If using coconut
milk, cut it with 50% cold water.

YOUR DAY IS HERE.
WAKE IT UP AND SHAKE IT UP WITH THESE.

CRUNCHY	FRUITY	FANCY	MILKY
Granola	Blackberries		
Goji	Raspberries		
Cacao	Strawberries	Maca	Almond
Toasted nuts: cashews, almonds, walnuts, pistachio	Banana	Spirulina	Hemp
	Kiwi	Moringa	Cashew
Toasted seeds: sunflower, pumpkin, flax	Mango	Reishi	Oat
	Pineapple	Ashwagandha	Coconut milk
Puffed cereal + grains: rice, amaranth, quinoa	Pomegranate	Activated charcoal	Coconut water
	Stone fruits		

ORANGE DATE MUESLI

SERVES 2

1 cup rolled oats
½ cup fresh orange juice
1½ cups creamy yogurt
3 dates, pitted and
   chopped

1 orange, skin and pith
   removed and chopped
2 tbsps currants

Mix all ingredients together. Transfer pudding to an airtight container and let soak overnight. Top with coconut flakes, fresh fruit, and / or nuts and seeds.

GOJI GRANOLA

MAKES 8 CUPS

2½ cups rolled oats
½ cup sesame seeds
½ cup quinoa
1 cup whole hemp seeds
½ tsp cinnamon
½ tsp cardamom

1 tsp kosher salt
½ cup olive oil
1 tsp vanilla extract
½ cup honey
¼ cup goji berries
½ cup dried apricots

Toss oats, sesame, quinoa, hemp seeds, cinnamon, cardamom, salt, olive oil, vanilla, and honey until thoroughly combined.

Spread in a thin single layer on baking sheets lined with parchment paper. Bake at 400 °F for 45 minutes or until lightly golden, stirring every 10-15 minutes.

Remove from the oven, transfer to a bowl, and stir in dried fruit. If you don't have goji or apricot any other dried fruits can be subbed in here. Once cooled, store in an airtight container for up to a month.

CACAO GRANOLA

MAKES 8 CUPS

½ cup chopped almonds
½ cup chopped cashews
1¼ cups whole hemp seeds
6 tbsps honey
1 tbsp coconut oil

¼ cup raw cacao powder
2 tbsps chia seeds
½ cup plus two tbsps dried coconut flakes
¼ tsp salt

Toss all ingredients in a medium mixing bowl.

Spread in a thin layer on baking sheets lined with parchment paper. Bake at 350 °F for about 10 minutes or until just sticky. Stir every couple of minutes.

Remove from oven. Let cool completely and break up with hands. Once completely cooled, store in an airtight container for up to a month. Don't pack this one up when warm or you'll end up with a brick.

SWEET PORRIDGE

SERVES 2

3 cups coconut milk	¼ cup fruit compote
1 cup water	¼ cup sweet potato purée
1 tbsp maple syrup	½ banana, sliced
1 tsp cardamom	2 tbsps chopped toasted
1 tsp ground ginger	pistachios
1 cup steel cut oats	

Bring coconut milk, water, maple syrup, and spices to a boil in a small stockpot. Add oats and reduce heat to a simmer. Cook until thickened and creamy, about 40 minutes.

Serve topped with compote, sweet potato purée, banana, and pistachio.

SWEET POTATO PURÉE

MAKES 2 CUPS

1 small sweet potato, roughly chopped	¼ cup coconut milk, plus more for desired consistency if needed
1 tsp salt	

Place sweet potato in a small saucepan and cover with water by 2 inches. Add salt. Bring to a boil, reduce heat to a simmer, and cook until very soft.

Drain potatoes and transfer to a food processor or blender. Add coconut milk and blend until completely smooth.

SIMPLE FRUIT COMPOTE

1 cup fruit (chopped into bite-sized pieces — if blueberries, raspberries, or blackberries, keep whole)	1 cup fresh orange juice
	1 tbsp fresh lemon juice
	¼ cup brown sugar
	½ tbsp ground ginger

Place all ingredients in a small saucepan over medium-high heat.

Simmer until fruit is very soft and thickened.

Remove from heat and let cool. Sauce will further thicken upon standing.

LOVE TOAST

SERVES 1

¼ cup tahini	1 tsp chopped mint
¼ cup berries	2 pieces whole grain toast
Honey to taste	or other toast of choice

Spread toast with tahini. Add berries, drizzle with honey to taste, and garnish with chopped mint

There's a hopeful smell of bacon

A little juice lends a hand

wafting through the air,

just at nose-level it seems.

Discussions of delayed trains from the aspirational breakfast meeting

bleed into the sparkly-eyed giggles

where the coffee does not.

Caffeine, sugar,

of rosy friends discussing lovers.

and some breakfast tacos

may help you forget...

...Your head hurts. The laundromat lost your favorite T-shirt and no one's texting you back. Some water would be nice.

E

M

Oh dear, you snoozed and snoozed again and now it's 10:33AM.

Not quite the up and at 'em you imagined.

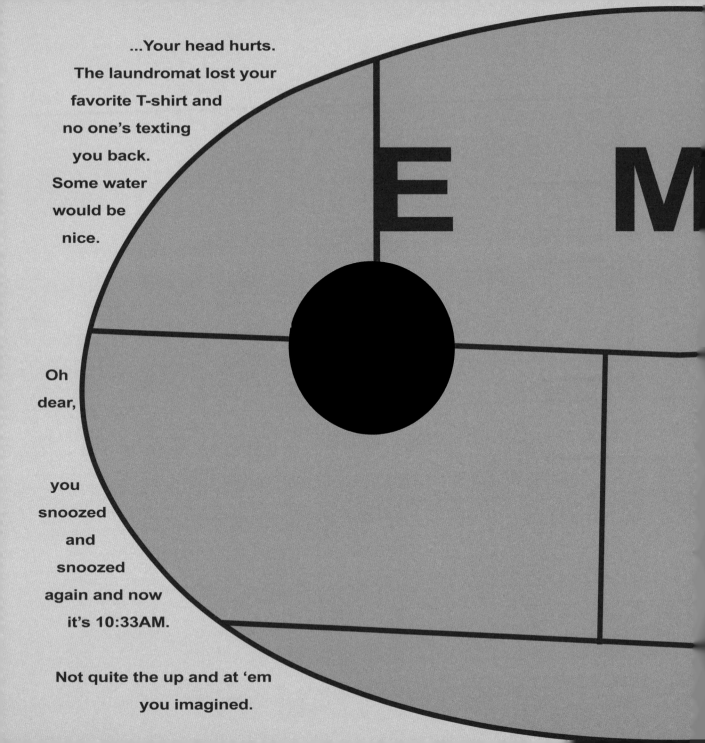

The rain is dreary,

but at least there are worms left for those birds

that took their time rising,

looking for, not finding, and finally purchasing

$5 umbrellas this morning.

Dozens of them make a soggy

sculpture near the door,

trace paths to the tables inside.

and squishy sneakers and slippery slides

10:33AM

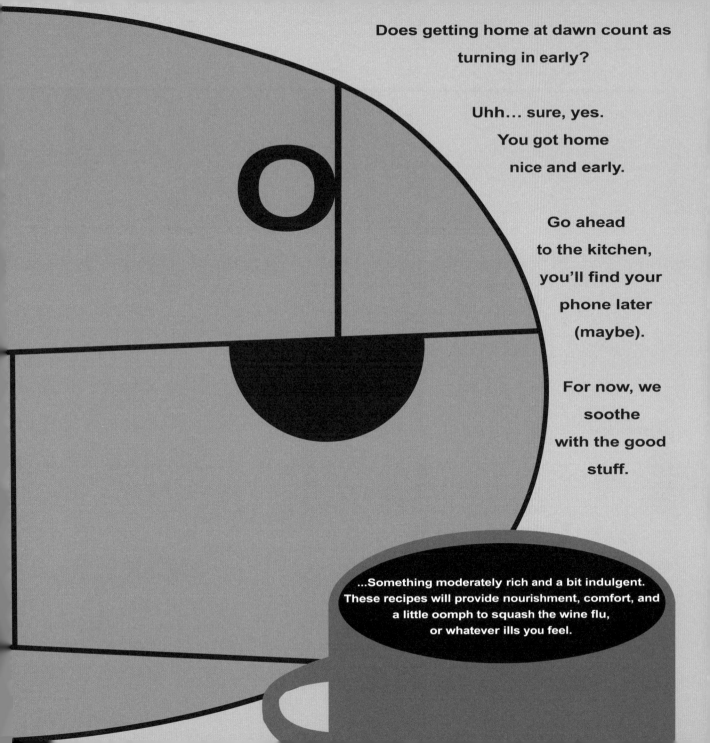

MATCHA BUTTERMILK PANCAKES

SERVES 2-3

1 ⅓ cups all purpose flour	2 eggs
3 tbsps sugar	1 ¼ cups buttermilk
1 tsp baking powder	2 tbsps melted butter
1 tsp kosher salt	Neutral oil or non-stick
3 tbsps matcha powder	cooking spray

Whisk dry ingredients together and set aside.

Whisk eggs, buttermilk, and butter together in a medium mixing bowl. Stir wet ingredients into dry until combined.

Heat a large non-stick skillet or griddle over medium-high heat. Add oil or non-stick cooking spray. Drop the batter into mounds onto the skillet. Cook until golden brown, flip, and cook through on the other side.

Serve with simple fruit compote (p 30), Goji granola (p 29), and pure maple syrup.

NORI-SESAME PANCAKES

SERVES 2-3

PANCAKES

2 cups bok choy, ½ inch of root end trimmed and finely chopped
2 cups kale — thick stems removed and finely chopped
3 tbsps ghee
⅔ cup whole wheat flour (or gluten-free flour of choice)
1 tbsp baking powder
1 egg
1 tbsp toasted sesame oil
½ tsp salt

½ tsp aleppo chili
⅔ cup coconut milk
¼ cup freshly squeezed lime juice
3 scallions, 2 finely chopped and 1 chopped into ½ inch pieces along the bias
¼ cup nori krinkles broken into small pieces, or nori sheets finely chopped
2 tbsps furikake
2 green thai chilies, minced
2 egg whites

SAUCE

4 tbsps tamari
4 tbsps mirin
1 tbsp fresh lime juice
1 tsp gochujang
1 tbsp rice vinegar
1 tbsp honey
½ tsp red chili flakes

1 garlic clove, grated
1 tbsp ginger root, grated
1 tbsp toasted sesame seeds
¼ cup cilantro leaves
Olive oil or good quality non-stick cooking spray

Boil 2 inches of salted water in a medium saucepan over high heat. Add bok choy and kale and cook, stirring, for a minute or two until just wilted. Strain well through a sieve and set aside.

Melt the ghee and place in a mixing bowl with the flour, baking powder, 1 whole egg, sesame oil, ½ teaspoon salt, aleppo, coconut milk, and lime juice.

Whisk, whisk, whisk. Fold in bok choy, kale, finely chopped scallions, nori, furikake, and green thai chilies.

Place the egg whites in a separate mixing bowl and whisk or beat with a hand mixer until soft peaks form. Gently fold the eggs into the batter.

Make dipping sauce: place all sauce ingredients except cilantro leaves in a small bowl. Stir, stir, stir.

Heat a large non-stick skillet or griddle over medium-high heat. Add olive oil or non-stick cooking spray.

Drop the batter into mounds on the skillet. Cook until golden brown, flip and cook through on the other side.

Garnish with cilantro leaves and remaining scallions. Serve with dipping sauce on the side.

A GOOD DAY STARTS
WITH A GOOD EGG

FRIED

SUNNY SIDE UP

SCRAMBLED

OVER EASY

OVER MEDIUM

OVER HARD

BREAKFAST TACOS

MAKES 2 TACOS

2 six inch tortillas
½ avocado, thinly sliced
1 tbsp butter or olive oil
4 eggs, scrambled
(add 2 tbsps milk for
extra creaminess
if desired)
3 tbsps cheddar, grated

2 tbsps mango salsa
(p 91)
2 tbsps diced tomatillo
¼ cup cilantro leaves
Dimes hot sauce (p 93)
to taste
Sea salt to taste

Warm tortillas in the oven or a dry sauté pan over medium heat.

Lay out your tortillas and add avocado, smashing and spreading it with a butter knife. Season with a little sea salt.

Heat butter or olive oil in a medium non-stick skillet. Add eggs, cheddar, and salt to taste and scramble until soft but not runny. No overcooked eggs or I'll appear out of thin air to slap your hand with a wooden spoon. Nicely cooked eggs should be yellow not brown.

Divide eggs between tortillas and top with mango salsa, tomatillo, and cilantro leaves. Douse with your fave hot sauce (Dimes obviously) until you can't see straight.

CHICKPEA STEW

Serves 2-3

2 tbsps coconut oil	1 pound collard greens
1 onion, thinly sliced	(or other hearty green),
4 garlic cloves,	thick stems removed,
thinly sliced	chopped into
2 thai chilies, minced	bite-sized pieces
1 tbsp ginger root, grated	½ cup lime juice
1 tsp fennel seeds	1 (24 oz) can whole peeled
2 tbsps yellow	tomatoes
curry powder	1 tsp salt
¼ tsp cayenne	½ tsp black pepper
4 cups cooked chickpeas	¼ cup chopped dill

In a small stockpot, sauté onion, garlic, chile, and ginger in coconut oil. Cook until softened. Add spices and cook a minute or two until fragrant.

Add chickpeas, greens, lime juice, and tomatoes with juices, tearing tomatoes with your hands as you add to break them apart a bit. Stir in salt and black pepper. Simmer until tomatoes are broken down and sauce has thickened, about 10 minutes.

Stir in dill just before serving.

SUGGESTIONS

This dish works great on its own as a hearty alternative breakfast dish. Beef it up with some avocado, and egg (hard boiled or sunny-side-up), or pulled chicken.

EGG FRIED RICE
WITH GOCHUJANG + KIMCHI

SERVES 2

½ cup good quality hoisin (such as Lee Kum Kee)
¼ cup good quality gochujang (such as Mother In Law's)
2 tsps brown sugar
¼ cup fresh lime juice
¼ cup rice vinegar
1 tbsp ginger, roughly chopped
4 garlic cloves
2 scallions — 1 finely chopped and 1 chopped into ½ inch pieces along the bias, divided
1 tbsp tamari
1 tsp sesame oil
¼ tsp cayenne
2 shiso leaves or 4 basil leaves
2 cups leftover cold rice
2 cups chopped leftover vegetables
½ cup chopped kimchi
2 eggs — cooked sunny-side-up
1 tbsp toasted sesame seeds
½ cup snow or snap peas cut in half on the bias
¼ cup cilantro leaves

MAKE SAUCE: Purée hoisin, gochujang, brown sugar, lime juice, rice vinegar, chopped ginger, garlic, ¾ of the chopped scallions, tamari, sesame oil, cayenne, and shiso in blender until very smooth.

Heat a large non-stick skillet with olive oil or butter over high heat. Add rice in a single layer and let cook undisturbed until brown and crispy on one side. Flip and cook until brown and crispy on the other side.

Add vegetables, kimchi, and two tablespoons sauce. Cook, breaking up rice with a wooden spoon until vegetables are heated through.

Serve fried rice topped with a sunny up egg, toasted sesame seeds, remaining scallions, snow peas, and cilantro. Serve with remaining sauce on the side.

NOON

12PM. The morning has gone, the late morning too. The minute and hour hands embrace for a one-minute visit to compare notes before returning to pacing, chasing. At high noon, a most kinetic hour, the orbits of the dining room intersect and harmonize in conversations and forkfuls.

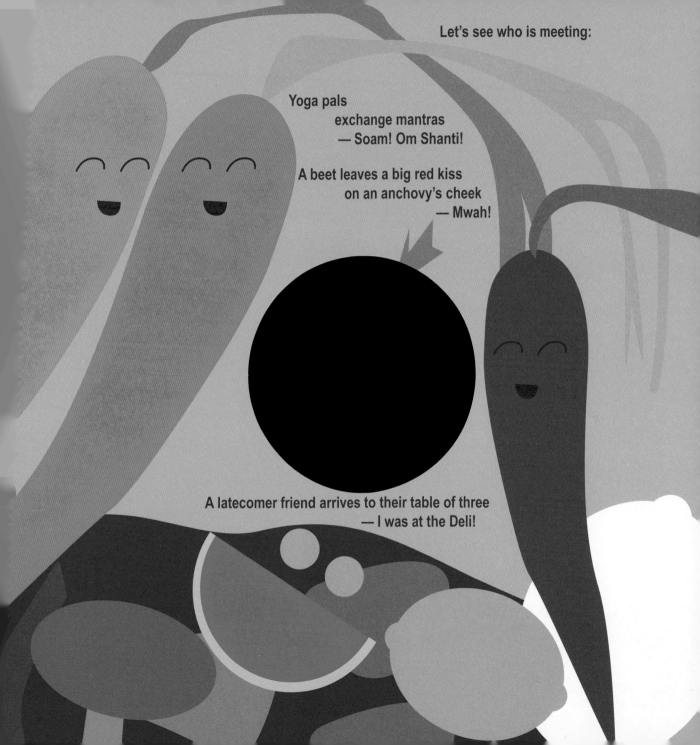

Let's see who is meeting:

Yoga pals
exchange mantras
— Soam! Om Shanti!

A beet leaves a big red kiss
on an anchovy's cheek
— Mwah!

A latecomer friend arrives to their table of three
— I was at the Deli!

...What were you doing last night?
In the grocery store. *What?* No, nice try.
It was *definitely you* in the freezer section.
Yes, you were wearing baggy sweatpants
and that shirt you stole from that *awful*
one-night-stand and you were *gaping*
at the Ben & Jerry's.
I *could hear* the
Sinead O'Connor
blasting
from your
headphones!
I kept calling your
name but you
couldn't hear me.
Anyway, *it was hilarious.*
— Oh stop being so sensitive.
You ate *how* much? *Hahahaha...*
Well, just go eat a salad.

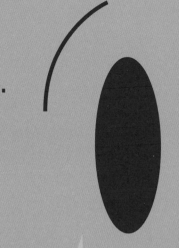

SALAD BAR

A Dimes salad is a major player in our essential lineup. A choose-your-own-adventure dream, salads set the stage to play with composition, texture, color, and palate through ingredients raw, roasted, chopped, crunchy, salty, sweet, and everything in between. They can be dressed up or down, simple or complex, warm or cold, topped with grilled meat or fish for a more complete meal, or served in palm-sized portions to accompany a bigger spread. A great salad is all about balance, containing a variety of flavors and textures while highlighting the best seasonal ingredients.

When building a salad, we usually have one or two ingredients in mind and then we layer from there. For the Winter Salad, we started with blood oranges—sweetly acidic and very juicy—so to balance this out we added some earthy beets. Cool, anisey raw fennel and tart gooseberries round out the sweetness of the beets and blood orange. For greens, we picked some nice hearty kale. Crunchy flax seeds impart texture and a pink peppercorn vinaigrette adds a burst of fiery acid pulling the dish together. Any leftover blood oranges and beets can be preserved in a chutney to throw over some veggies in a grain bowl or on top of some roasted chicken or fish. Fennel can be pickled and saved for future salads or a crunchy snack.

Salads are an integral part of conscious eating, providing the perfect opportunity to practice a more mindful approach in the kitchen. Cooking habits that are strongly rooted in a variety of vegetables and grains that help to nourish and restore. Tune your receptors, listen to your body, respond in kind, and be rewarded by aligning with your sensitive spirit.

SPRING

SUMMER

FALL

WINTER

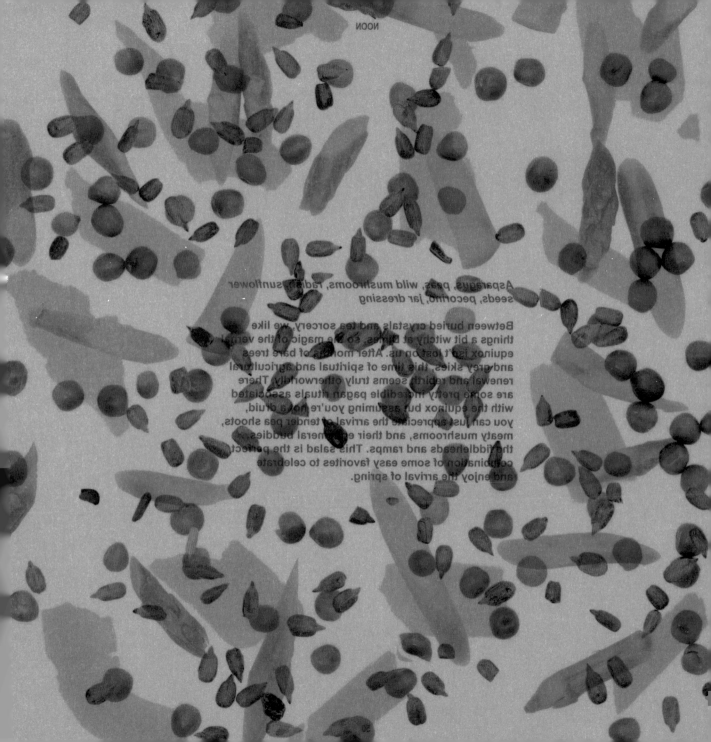

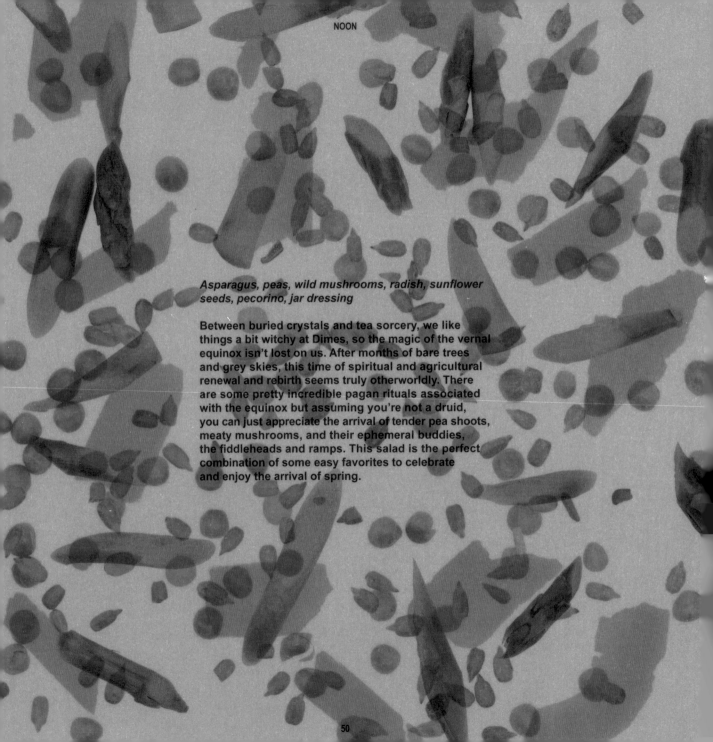

*Asparagus, peas, wild mushrooms, radish, sunflower
seeds, pecorino, jar dressing*

Between buried crystals and tea sorcery, we like
things a bit witchy at Dimes, so the magic of the vernal
equinox isn't lost on us. After months of bare trees
and grey skies, this time of spiritual and agricultural
renewal and rebirth seems truly otherworldly. There
are some pretty incredible pagan rituals associated
with the equinox but assuming you're not a druid,
you can just appreciate the arrival of tender pea shoots,
meaty mushrooms, and their ephemeral buddies,
the fiddleheads and ramps. This salad is the perfect
combination of some easy favorites to celebrate
and enjoy the arrival of spring.

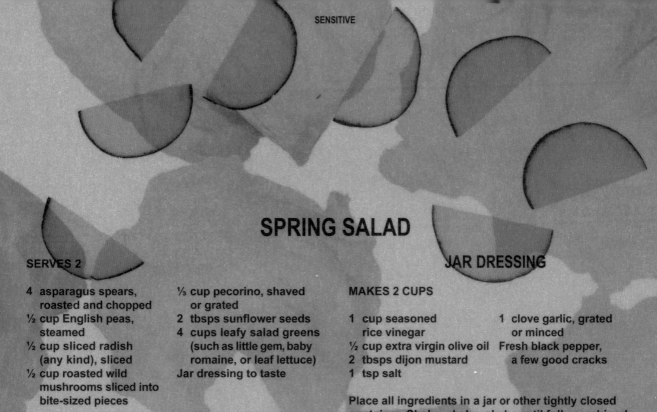

SPRING SALAD

SERVES 2

4 asparagus spears, roasted and chopped
½ cup English peas, steamed
½ cup sliced radish (any kind), sliced
½ cup roasted wild mushrooms sliced into bite-sized pieces

⅓ cup pecorino, shaved or grated
2 tbsps sunflower seeds
4 cups leafy salad greens (such as little gem, baby romaine, or leaf lettuce)
Jar dressing to taste

Place salad leaves and radish in a large mixing bowl and drizzle with freshly shaken jar dressing. Gently toss the leaves with tongs or hands until all leaves are lightly coated. Season with a little salt and pepper. Toss in the rest of the ingredients and add a little more dressing if needed.

Serve in your favorite bowl and enjoy.

JAR DRESSING

MAKES 2 CUPS

1 cup seasoned rice vinegar
½ cup extra virgin olive oil
2 tbsps dijon mustard
1 tsp salt

1 clove garlic, grated or minced
Fresh black pepper, a few good cracks

Place all ingredients in a jar or other tightly closed container. Shake, shake, shake until fully combined.

Seasonal add in:
Chopped ramps, about 2 tablespoons.

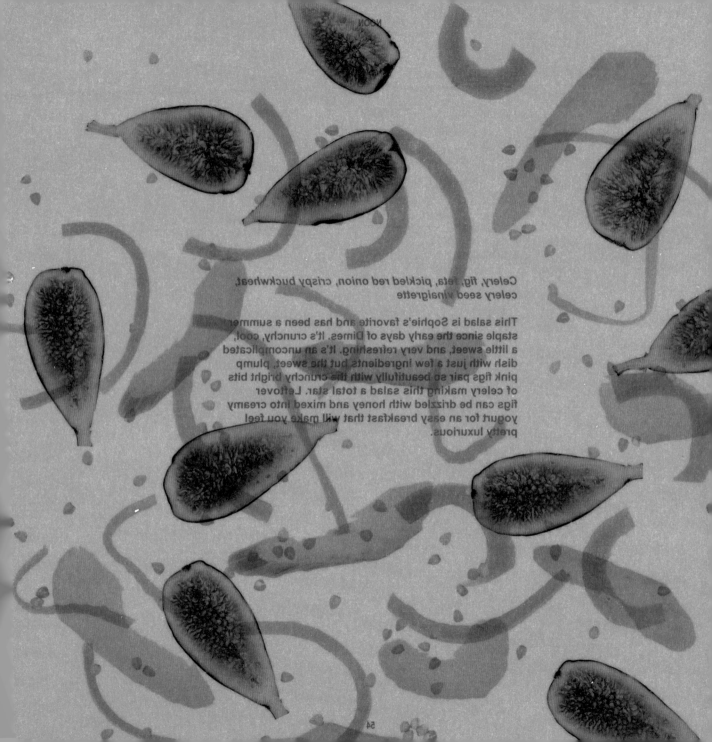

Celery, fig, feta, pickled red onion, crispy buckwheat, celery seed vinaigrette

This salad is Sophie's favorite and has been a summer staple since the early days of Dimes. It's crunchy, cool, a little sweet, and very refreshing. It's an uncomplicated dish with just a few ingredients but the sweet, plump pink figs pair so beautifully with the crunchy bright bits of celery making this salad a total star. Leftover figs can be drizzled with honey and mixed into creamy yogurt for an easy breakfast that will make you feel pretty luxurious.

SUMMER SALAD

CELERY SEED VINAIGRETTE

SERVES 2

2 tbsps buckwheat groats
4 cups baby salad greens
½ cup celery, chopped
6 figs, stems trimmed and
cut in quarters

2 tbsps pickled red onion
¼ cup crumbled feta
Celery seed vinaigrette
to taste

Place everything in a large mixing bowl. Drizzle
lightly with celery seed vinaigrette. Baby greens are
very delicate so make sure not to over dress — it's
easy to add more dressing but impossible to take it
away. Taste and add more dressing if needed.
Season with a little salt and pepper.

Serve in your favorite bowl and enjoy.

MAKES 2 CUPS

1 shallot
1 garlic clove
½ tbsp dijon
¼ cup lemon juice
¼ cup apple cider vinegar
½ tbsp celery seeds

1 tsp fennel seeds
¼ cup basil leaves
½ tsp salt
½ cup high quality
neutral oil
½ cup extra virgin olive oil

Blend everything except oil in a blender until smooth.
With the motor running, add oil in a very, very slow and
steady stream to emulsify.

CELERY SEED VINAIGRETTE

tbsp dijon
¼ cup extra virgin olive

Blend everything except oil in a blender until
With the motor running, add oil in a very, very
steady stream to emulsify.

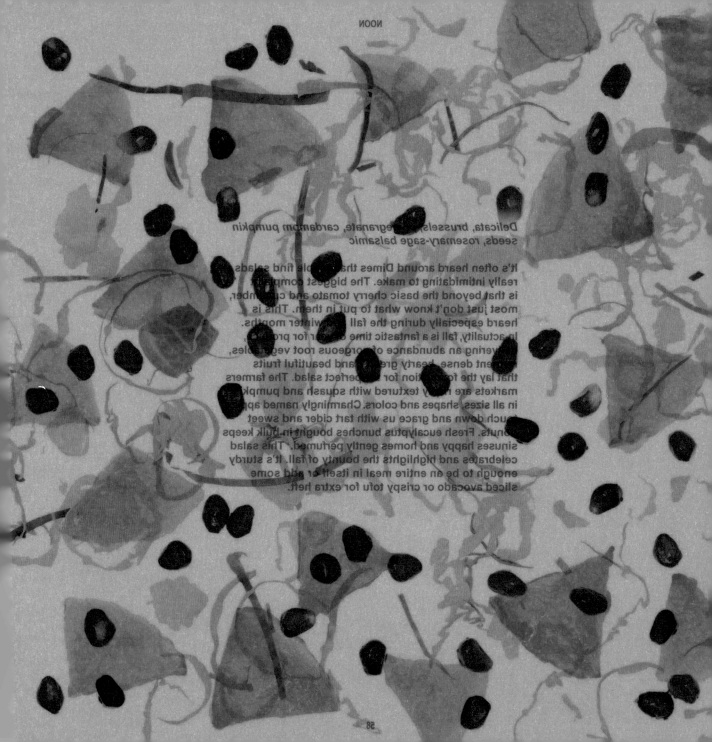

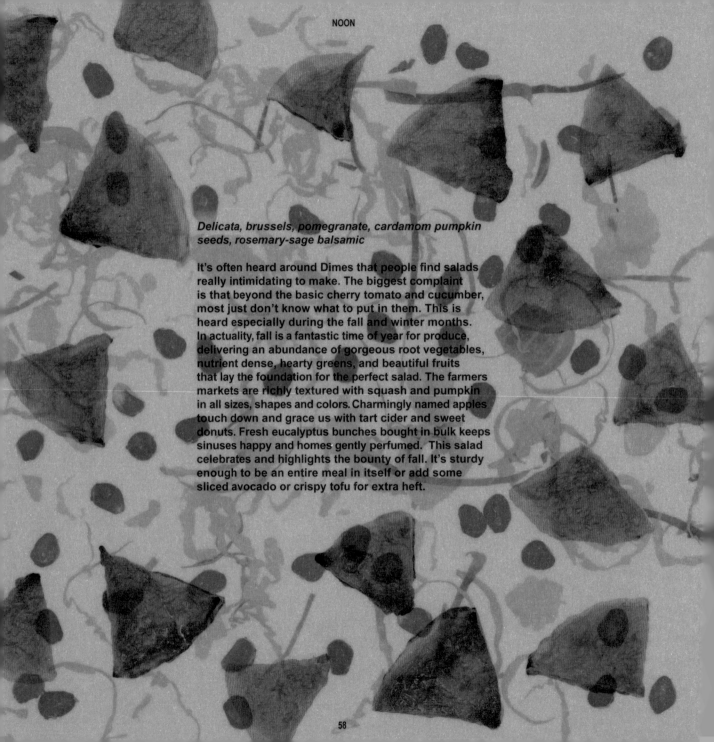

Delicata, brussels, pomegranate, cardamom pumpkin seeds, rosemary-sage balsamic

It's often heard around Dimes that people find salads really intimidating to make. The biggest complaint is that beyond the basic cherry tomato and cucumber, most just don't know what to put in them. This is heard especially during the fall and winter months. In actuality, fall is a fantastic time of year for produce, delivering an abundance of gorgeous root vegetables, nutrient dense, hearty greens, and beautiful fruits that lay the foundation for the perfect salad. The farmers markets are richly textured with squash and pumpkin in all sizes, shapes and colors. Charmingly named apples touch down and grace us with tart cider and sweet donuts. Fresh eucalyptus bunches bought in bulk keeps sinuses happy and homes gently perfumed. This salad celebrates and highlights the bounty of fall. It's sturdy enough to be an entire meal in itself or add some sliced avocado or crispy tofu for extra heft.

FALL SALAD

SERVES 2

1 small delicata squash (about 8oz), or other fall squash, chopped
1 tbsp maple syrup
⅛ tsp cayenne
½ tsp salt plus more to taste
2 tbsps toasted pumpkin seeds
1 tbsp plus ½ tsp olive oil

½ tsp cardamom
4 cups baby mustard greens or other hearty salad green
1 ½ cups brussels sprouts, thinly shaved on mandolin or sliced with a knife
½ cup pomegranate seeds
Rosemary-sage balsamic to taste

Delicata squash skin is edible. Toss chopped squash with maple syrup, cayenne, ½ teaspoon salt, and 1 tablespoon olive oil. Roast until tender and lightly golden.

Toss pumpkin seeds with ½ teaspoon olive oil and cardamom.

Place greens and brussels sprouts in a medium mixing bowl. Drizzle with rosemary-sage balsamic. Gently toss the leaves with tongs or hands until all leaves are lightly coated. Season with a little salt and pepper.

Divide greens between two plates. Scatter with delicata squash, pomegranate, and pumpkin seeds.

ROSEMARY-SAGE BALSAMIC

MAKES 2 CUPS

¾ cup balsamic vinegar
2 tbsps dijon mustard
3 cloves garlic
1 shallot
2 tbsps rosemary, roughly chopped
2 tbsps sage, roughly chopped

1 ½ tbsps fresh orange juice
½ tsp salt
Fresh black pepper, a couple of cracks
½ cup high quality neutral oil
½ cup extra virgin olive oil

Blend everything except oil in a blender until smooth. With the motor running, add oil in a very, very slow and steady stream to emulsify.

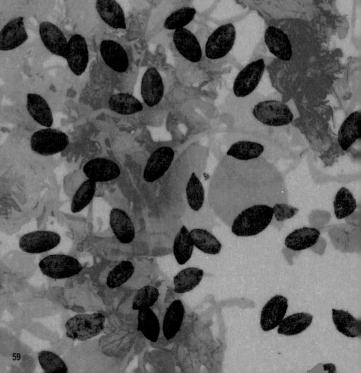

FALL SALAD

SERVES 2

ROSEMARY-SAGE BALSAMIC

MAKES 2 CUPS

1 small delicata squash (about 8oz.), or other fall squash, chopped

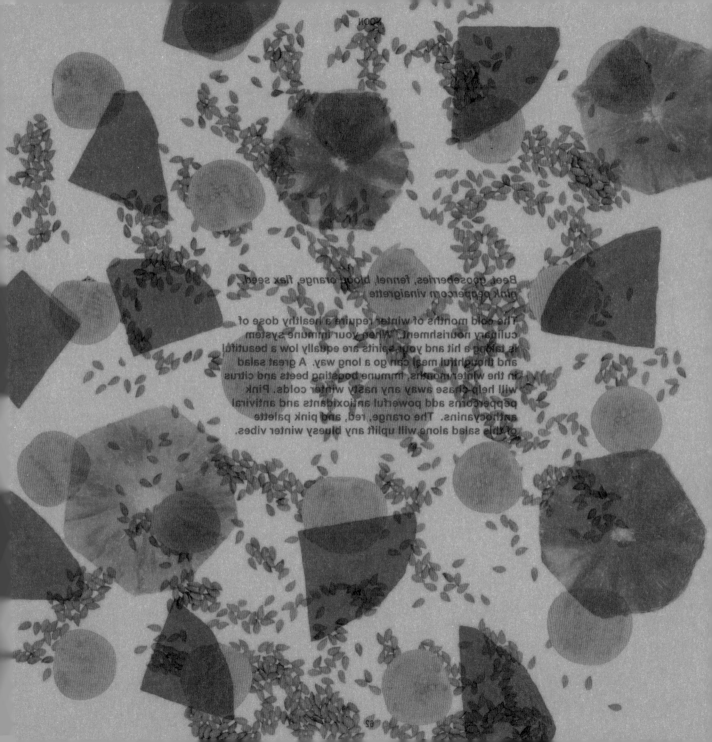

Beet, gooseberries, fennel, blood orange, flax seed, pink peppercorn vinaigrette

The cold months of winter require a healthy dose of culinary nourishment. When your immune system is taking a hit and your spirits are equally low a beautiful and thoughtful meal can go a long way. A great salad in the winter months, immune boosting beets and citrus will help chase away any nasty winter colds. Pink peppercorns add powerful antioxidants and antiviral anthocyanins. The orange, red, and pink palette of this salad alone will uplift any bluesy winter vibes.

Beet, gooseberries, fennel, blood orange, flax seed,
pink peppercorn vinaigrette

The cold months of winter require a healthy dose of
culinary nourishment. When your immune system
is taking a hit and your spirits are equally low a beautiful
and thoughtful meal can go a long way. A great salad
in the winter months, immune boosting beets and citrus
will help chase away any nasty winter colds. Pink
peppercorns add powerful antioxidants and antiviral
anthocyanins. The orange, red, and pink palette
of this salad alone will uplift any bluesy winter vibes.

WINTER SALAD

SERVES 2

1 small beet, roughly
   5 oz, scrubbed but
   not peeled
½ cup apple cider vinegar
1 tbsp salt
Optional: bay leaf, herbs
   (rosemary + thyme work
   best here), garlic clove,
   ginger, aromatic spices
   i.e. peppercorns, star
   anise, cinnamon sticks)

Gooseberries,
   a handful
¼ of a small fennel bulb
2 blood oranges
1 tbsp flax seeds
4 cups kale (any kind),
   thick stems removed
   and chopped into bite-
   sized pieces
Pink peppercorn
   vinaigrette to taste

Put the beet in a small saucepan along with enough
water to cover it and add apple cider vinegar, and
1 tablespoon salt. Add optional (any or all) add-ins if
using. Bring water to a boil and turn down the heat
to a simmer. Cook until the beet is fork tender. Remove
beet from the water and let it cool. Peel it and dice it.

Peel papery skins from the gooseberries and cut them
in half through the stem end.

Cut fennel into ¼ inch wedges. Use a mandolin if
you're brave. Set aside remaining fennel to enjoy
later either fresh, pickled, or roasted.

Remove skin and pith from oranges. Cut first into
¼ inch rounds, horizontally then cut those in half
to make half moons.

Dress it. Place kale and shaved fennel in a bowl and
drizzle with pink peppercorn vinaigrette. Massage
it with the dressing until kale begins to soften and all
the leaves are coated well. Season with a little salt
and pepper. Toss in the rest of the ingredients and
add a little more dressing if needed.

Serve in your favorite bowl and enjoy.

PINK PEPPERCORN VINAIGRETTE

MAKES 2 CUPS

1 shallot
1 garlic clove
½ tbsp dijon mustard
¼ cup grapefruit juice
½ tsp salt
½ cup extra virgin olive oil

1 tbsp pink peppercorns
1 tbsp orange blossom
   water
¼ cup white wine vinegar
½ cup high quality
   neutral oil

Blend everything except oil in a blender until smooth.
With the motor running, add oil in a very, very slow
and steady stream to emulsify.

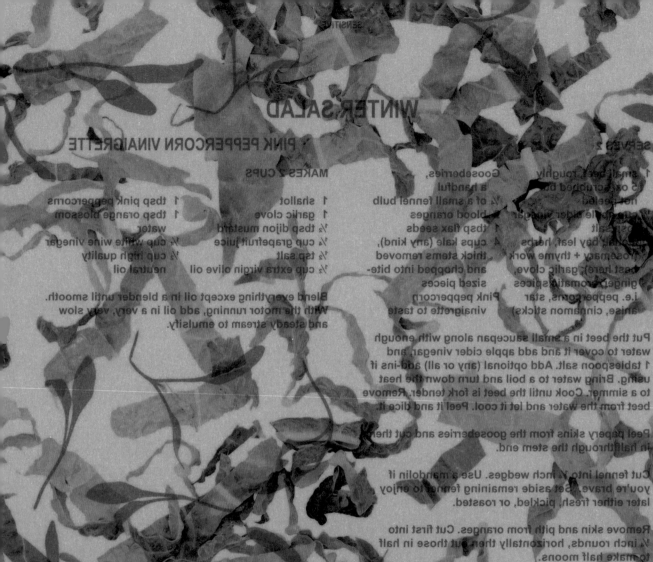

SERVES 2

PINK PEPPERCORN VINAIGRETTE

Dress it. Place kale and shaved fennel in a bowl and drizzle with pink peppercorn vinaigrette. Massage it with the dressing until kale begins to soften and all the leaves are coated well. Season with a little salt and pepper. Toss in the rest of the ingredients and add a little more dressing if needed.

Serve in your favorite bowl and enjoy.

THE FIVE ELEMENTS FOR A COSMIC SALAD CREATION
For a stellar salad, pick one from each category and toss with your favorite dressing.
Choose wisely, and blast into the fourth dimension.

GREENS	RAW	COOKED	CRUNCHY	PICKLED
Broccoli leaf	Pomegranate	Squash	Sunflower seeds	Red Onion
Kale	Apple	Sweet potato	Pepitas	Mustard seeds
Cabbage	Hakurei turnips	Beets	Kasha	Raisins
Collards	Watermelon	Green beans	Flax seeds	Cabbage
Chards	Pears	Carrots	Almonds	Rhubarb
Arugula	Stonefruit	Celery root	Hazelnuts	Watermelon
Mizuna	Figs	Cauliflower	Dukkah	Cauliflower
Spinach	Fennel	Broccoli	Pistachio	Cucumber
Baby lettuces	Kohlrabi	Zucchini	Walnuts	Fennel
Sorrel	Cucumber	Eggplant	Cashews	Carrots
Frisee	Citrus	Corn	Croutons	Beets
Escarole	Gooseberries	Asparagus	Breadcrumbs	Peppers
Radicchio	Cabbage	Mushrooms	Pine nuts	Fresno chili
Mustard Greens	Radish	Peas	Sesame seeds	Jalapeno
Romaine	Tomatoes	Brussels sprouts	Hemp seeds	Mushrooms
Butter lettuce	Celery	Rhubarb	Peanuts	Green beans

3:00PM

At 3PM, diners dwindle, drinkers linger. In just an hour, the kitchen will close, yet as that time draws nearer, servers, bartenders and cooks double, clock-hands passing, one chasing the other.

The day's team doesn't just sweep up the crumbs of breakfast and lunch. Before they leave, they fill what's empty — sauce, sugar, paper and wine — to be put to use by the team tapping in. At the evening's end, it will happen again. Sow now, reap later.

Do you close for an hour? Juice a lemon in the morning to squeeze onto the evening's greens? Does yesterday's you consider now's you? And now's you, the future you too?

ASPIRATIONAL

...You, living your dream life. Get up, grab that magic juice that will cleanse your kidneys and give you perfect hair. Strap on those $400 shoes (worth it) and that $10 bag (it's all about balance) You better move it if you're going to get to yoga before your date (dim sum then the Met) Have an exit plan just in case (I think the crew is going to Dimes tonight) but if it goes well you can roll up together later for karaoke.

We want you to use this book like a roadmap, meandering through the Dimes world at your own pace. Stopping off where it suits, taking in the view. Meals should reflect this dreamy and organic approach, using what you have on hand, making it work for you. Being playful, being bold, mixing and matching your salads and grains. Doing what makes you happy, taking chances, connecting the puzzle pieces.

Aspiration is individual. Everyone has their own unique roadmap with many different paths that lead to the final destination. For some, it's about climbing the highest mountain, for others it's about climbing the highest ladder.

Here we show you how one day of heavy lifting in the kitchen can feed you well for a week, giving you nourishment and freeing up time to devote to your own aspirations, in whatever form they take.

VEGETABLES

An easy trick to maintaining a healthy diet is to cook up a big variety of seasonal vegetables and grains to use throughout the week. Roasted sweet potato wedges can be mashed for tomorrow's dinner or puréed for our porridge recipe. Leftover quinoa can be reheated and renewed by stirring in some pesto or eaten cold tossed into a green salad. Leftover rice and veggies can be used to make our Egg Fried Rice (p 41).

Let's be real — we're living full lives that involve late days at work (often taking that work home with us), little kids at home (who are hungry and missing our faces), and packed social lives (that need extra attention due to neglect in favor of the latest TV binge). After these long, involved days, we still need to eat but often don't feel like cooking. That said, it's so important to eat a healthy and balanced diet to keep up the energy and stamina we need to thrive in our jam-packed aspirational existences. In order to accomplish this more easily at home, you can rely on the practices employed in professional kitchens. At Dimes, when we are getting ready to serve hundreds of people throughout the week, we need to be prepared behind the scenes. We set ourselves up for success by prepping all our products ahead of time, so that it's fast and easy to turn them into a plated dish. No one wants to wait an hour for their food. These practices are equally useful to the home cook and cut down greatly on the amount of meal prep you need to do when you come home from a long day at work.

You can set yourself up for the week by doing some of the hard labor as soon as you bring groceries home by immediately prepping the items that take the most time and elbow grease. Wash and chop your kale and keep it in a reusable produce bag in the fridge. Then you'll always have kale ready to be quickly sautéed, steamed, or tossed into a smoothie. Immediately soak some chickpeas so there's no stress once dinner rolls around. You can also pre-cut sturdier vegetables like winter squash, sweet potatoes, and cauliflower so that all you need to do is throw them on a roasting pan. Just make sure to eat any pre-cut vegetables within three to four days or so because cut vegetables don't keep as long. If they do sit around a little longer than anticipated, you can probably just pickle them. Finally, throw together a big batch of pesto so you have a good healthy sauce to put on everything. A little planning goes a long way.

RAW

Many vegetables can be enjoyed raw. Eating foods raw keeps their nutritional content intact and increases the bioavailability of these nutrients. Raw or lightly cooked foods are generally the most healthful. Don't be afraid to mix raw and cooked foods in one dish. The contrast of texture and flavor creates a beautiful complexity.

SAUTÉ

Sauté your tender vegetables or hearty greens. Heat a little oil in a sauté pan. Extra virgin olive oil and coconut oil works well. Add vegetables.

Season with salt to taste. Toss frequently and cook until tender. Greens only need a couple of minutes, cut vegetables need a little longer, usually around 6-8 minutes.

ROASTING

Roast at 400 °F. Cut your veggies into bite-sized pieces and place in a mixing bowl. Use enough oil to lightly coat each piece. Extra virgin olive oil, avocado oil, and coconut oil all work well. If coconut oil is solid, let soften in a warm place before using.

Salt. Season generously but don't overdo it. Understand the vegetable you're working with. Hearty vegetables like hard squash and potatoes need more salt than tender asparagus or summer squash. Hold your hand at least 12 inches above your bowl and scatter salt evenly over the top. Seasoning from high up ensures even distribution. Toss to combine.

Spread your vegetables across the sheet pan in an even layer with some space between each piece. Don't overcrowd your pans — vegetables piled on top of each other or too close together will steam instead of roasting.

Roast according to the guideline on the right. Vegetables are done when just tender and a little browned around the edges. Keep in mind, the smaller you cut your veggies, the shorter the cooking time. The following guidelines are based on bite-sized pieces, roughly one inch in size. Veggies should still have a little bite to them — this helps keep them nutritionally intact. Vegetables lose nutrients the longer they are cooked and the higher the heat.

ROOTS check at 30 minutes. Cook longer if needed. Beets * potatoes * carrots * parsnips * sweet potatoes

HARD SQUASH check at 30 minutes. Cook longer if needed. Some take up to an hour. Butternut * acorn * kabocha * pumpkin

CRUCIFEROUS FRIENDS 15 minutes Broccoli * brussels sprouts * romanesco * cauliflower

TOMATOES 15-20 minutes Remove stems and roast whole until skin begins to shrivel and they start to burst.

THE REST 10-15 minutes Zucchini * asparagus * yellow squash * green beans * peppers * mushrooms

STEAM

Works for all vegetable friends. Cut vegetables into bite-sized pieces and set aside.

Place an inch or two of water in a saucepan. Place steamer basket on top. Water should not touch the basket. Bring to a boil. Reduce heat to a simmer.

Add vegetables to basket. Spread in an even layer. Cover with a lid. Cook until tender with a little bite.

Season with salt and pepper, some lemon juice, or a fresh sauce.

OOPS I OVERCOOKED MY VEGETABLES

Purée your roots and hard veggies in the blender and sell it as fanciness. Enjoy alongside your other veggies, grains, and proteins. Add some coconut milk for creaminess.

Purée your tender veggies, add some stock, coconut milk or water, and fresh herbs if you have them. Season with lemon juice, salt, and pepper. Now you have a lovely soup.

PARTY WITH GRAINS. A GUIDE.

When cooking your grains, there are a few really easy ways to boost flavor and healthfulness.

Cook any of the grains in stock (vegetable, beef, chicken or fish depending on your current feelings and menu planning) to build flavor.

Add aromatics for increased depth of flavor. See our guide on page 80.

For nutty richness, toast your grains in ghee, coconut oil, or olive oil before adding water.

Don't forget the salt. About a teaspoon per dry cup of grains.

Here's a general guideline to cooking our favorite grains. That said, it's always a good idea to check the bag or box of the brand you're using since there are sometimes variations in the product that affect ratios and cooking times.

GRAIN	WET:DRY	METHOD	TIME	YIELD
Barley	3:1	Bring to a boil, cover + simmer	40-60 min	3.5x
Black rice	2:1	Bring to a boil, cover + simmer *	35 min	3x
Brown rice	2.5:1	Bring to a boil, cover + simmer *	20-40 min	3x
Bulgur	2:1	Bring to a boil, cover + simmer	10-12 min	3x
Couscous	2:1	Bring water to a boil, stir grain, cover, remove from heat. Let sit five minutes. Fluff with a fork.	5 min	3x
Farro	6:1	Rinse farro under cold water. Cook like pasta until al dente. Drain through a sieve.	20-40 min	3x
Freekeh	2:1	Bring to a boil, cover + simmer	15-25 min	3x
Quinoa	2:1	Bring to a boil, cover + simmer	15 min	3x
Wild rice	3:1	Bring to a boil, cover + simmer	40-60 min	3.5x

Or just use a rice cooker. Why make it harder on yourself?

WILD RICE

WITH STONE FRUIT, PROSCIUTTO + LAVENDER PISTACHIO VINAIGRETTE

SERVES 2

2 cups wild rice, cooked al dente

4 tbsps lavender pistachio vinaigrette (p 95)

1 tbsp fresh lemon juice

½ tsp salt

Fresh black pepper, a few cracks

¼ cup chopped mint

1 ripe peach, or plum, skin on, pit removed, and cut into wedges

15 cherries, pitted, stems removed and cut in half

3 celery stalks, cut into ¼ inch pieces across the rib

2 tbsps pickled red onion

4 slices prosciutto, torn length-wise into ½ inch wide ribbons (optional)

2 tbsps chopped, toasted pistachios

Place wild rice in a medium mixing bowl. Drizzle with vinaigrette and lemon juice and add salt and pepper. Using your hands, massage the grains with the dressing until thoroughly coated. Add in mint, stone fruit, celery, and pickled red onion and toss to combine. Divide between two bowls. Top with prosciutto ribbons (if using) and garnish with chopped pistachio.

FREEKEH PILAF

WITH KALE, KOHLRABI + WILD MUSHROOMS

SERVES 2

2 cups cooked freekeh

2 tbsps fresh lemon juice

1 tbsp good quality extra virgin olive oil

1 tbsp pomegranate molasses

¼ tsp red pepper flakes

½ tsp salt

Fresh black pepper, a few cracks

¼ cup chopped mint

2 tbsps toasted pumpkin seeds

1 tsp toasted fennel seeds

2 tbsps pickled raisins

1 cups sautéed kale (optional: sauté with a little sliced garlic)

½ cup thinly sliced kohlrabi

½ cup roasted wild mushrooms

Place freekeh in a medium mixing bowl. Add lemon juice, olive oil, pomegranate molasses, red pepper flakes, salt, and pepper. Using your hands, massage the grains with the dressing until thoroughly coated. Add remaining ingredients and toss to combine. Divide between two bowls.

BARLEY
WITH ZUCCHINI, ASPARAGUS, PECORINO + OLIVES

SERVES 2

2 cups barley, cooked
2 tbsps tahini vinaigrette
   (p 95), plus more to taste
1 tbsp fresh lemon juice
½ tsp salt, plus more
   to taste
Fresh black pepper,
   a few cracks
1 cup asparagus, roasted
   and chopped into ½ inch
   pieces on the bias

1 cup zucchini,
   roasted and diced
   into ½ inch pieces
½ cup sliced green olives
   (We love Castelvetrano)
¼ cup chopped mint
¼ cup chopped parsley
2 tbsps dried currants
½ cup pecorino, shaved

Place barley in a medium mixing bowl. Drizzle with
vinaigrette and lemon juice and add salt and pepper.
Using your hands, massage the grains with the
dressing until thoroughly coated. Add remaining
ingredients and toss to combine. Divide between
two bowls.

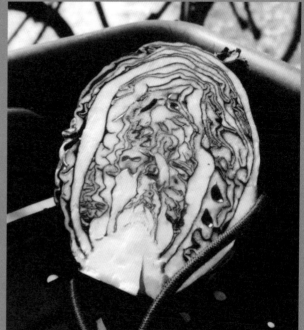

BULGUR
WITH SPICED EGGPLANT, LABNEH + DUKKAH

SERVES 2

2 Japanese eggplants (or other small eggplant, such as graffiti or other heirloom varieties)	1 cup bulgur, cooked
	1 tbsp dill, chopped
	1 tsp lemon juice
	½ tsp sumac
¼ cup aromatic spice blend at room temperature	½ tsp salt
	2 tbsps labneh
	2 tbsps cashew dukkah

Trim stems from eggplant and slice in half length-wise. Using a paring knife make diagonal slashes about 1 inch deep and 1 inch apart down the length of the cut side. Do not cut through skin. Repeat, making new crosswise slashes in the other direction to create a diamond pattern.

Using a pastry brush, spread the aromatic spice blend across the eggplants, completely covering the cut side in a thin layer. Repeat.

Place the eggplants cut side up in a roasting pan. Roast at 400 °F until very tender.

Meanwhile, toss the bulgur with dill, lemon juice, sumac, and salt.

Divide eggplant between two plates, top with bulgur, add a dollop of labneh and garnish with dukkah.

AROMATIC SPICE BLEND

MAKES 1 ½ CUPS

1 cup extra virgin olive oil	2 tsps ground fennel
2 oranges, zest only	4 tsps paprika
2 lemons, zest only	½ tbsp ground cinnamon
4 garlic cloves	1 tsp ground nutmeg
3 tbsps ground cumin	1 tsp aleppo chili flakes
1 tsps ground cardamom	1 tsp salt

Purée all ingredients in a blender until completely smooth. Store in the fridge for up to 3 months.

CASHEW DUKKAH

MAKES 1 ½ CUPS

1 cup toasted cashews	2 tbsps coriander seeds, toasted
¼ cup sesame seeds, toasted	2 tbsps cumin seeds, toasted
1 tsp black peppercorns	

Coarsely grind in a blender or spice grinder. Make sure nuts and spices are completely cooled before grinding or you'll end up with spiced cashew butter.

BASIC RISOTTO

SERVES 2

3 tbsps butter	4 cups vegetable stock
2 shallots, finely chopped	1 tsp salt
2 garlic cloves, minced	½ tsp black pepper
1 ½ cups Arborio rice	¼ cup parmigiana, finely
1/2 cup dry white wine	grated

Melt butter in a medium stockpot over low heat. Add shallots and garlic and sauté until translucent and very tender being careful not to brown. No "raw" onion taste should remain.

Add rice and toast, stirring, until fragrant.

Add wine, and reduce until liquid is evaporated.

Add 1 cup of vegetable stock along with salt and pepper and reduce until liquid is evaporated, stirring frequently. Repeat, adding 1 cup of stock at a time, until rice is cooked through and texture is creamy with almost all liquid evaporated. Fold in cheese.

VARIATIONS. UPGRADE YOUR BASIC.

GRAINS. Sub farro, barley, or quinoa for rice. Farro should be rinsed with cold water before cooking.

VEGAN. Sub olive oil for butter and nutritional yeast for parmigiana for vegan risotto.

MISO. Add a tablespoon white miso along with butter or olive oil for umami.

LEMON. Add 3 tablespoons fresh lemon juice along with the cheese for lemon risotto.

VEGETABLES WELCOME

Fold in some vegetables + herbs to elevate your risotto, here are some good combos:

Maitake mushrooms + kale + chopped thyme + basic farro

Butternut squash + shiitake mushrooms + chopped sage + miso quinoa

Swiss chard + roasted grapes + rosemary + vegan barley

Asparagus + English peas + parsley + lemon basic arborio

Following the basic recipe, add about 2 cups cooked vegetables and 1 tablespoon herbs. Fold cooked vegetables in at the end. If using thyme, sage or rosemary, add along with the onions and garlic. If parsley, fold in at the end just before serving.

AROMATHERAPY

AROMATICS

Cooking is a sensory experience. Eyes take in color and form. Ears listen to the rolling, gentle simmer of the stockpot and the sharp, crackling sound of the frying pan. Hands peel papery skins and pick soft leaves. Our tongues detect sweet notes and briny tangs. Our noses lead us to discover whatever magic lies beneath the lid.

Keep loose tea bags on hand and use for aromatic sachets that can be easily removed at the end of cooking. Cheesecloth tied with natural twine also works well. Nutmilk bags will work too. Add 5-7 sprigs of herbs and/or a tablespoon of spices in with your grains while they're cooking. Remove at the end with kitchen tongs or a spoon. Fresh elements can be added in and strained off through a sieve at the end. Add fermented ingredients 1 tablespoon at a time to taste.

HERBS	SPICES	FRESH	FERMENTED
Parsley	Black peppercorn	Fennel fronds	Kimchi paste
Sage	Cinnamon	Ginger root	Miso
Rosemary	Star anise	Turmeric root	Gochujang
Thyme	Fennel seeds	Lemongrass	Garlic paste
Bay leaf	Coriander seeds	Citrus peel	Umeboshi
Lime leaf	Cloves	Garlic	Fish sauce
Avocado leaf	Whole cardamom	Onion	Tamari

BEANS AND LEGUMES

Let's break it down.

Soak. Dried beans should be soaked overnight both to shorten cooking time and, more importantly, to reduce the amount of phytic acid present which can impair the bodies absorption of important minerals like iron and calcium. This also helps to reduce the toots.

Don't soak lentils.

Rinse. Once your beans have been thoroughly soaked, rinse under cold running water and pick through for any stray stones or other natural debris.

Place in a stockpot covered with several inches (about 4-5) of fresh cold water and a good amount of salt.

Add your aromatics. What works well for grains also works for beans.

Watch your heat. Bring your water to a gentle simmer rather than a boil. If the water is too hot, the beans will burst and won't cook evenly. A gentle simmer will result in tender, in tact, and evenly cooked beans. Different beans have different cooking times. Check out our chart below for a few of our favorites.

Freeze your cooking liquid and use like vegetable stock.

TYPE	DRY AMOUNT	COOKING TIME	YIELD
Anasazi bean	1 cup	60 min	2x
Black bean	1 cup	60-90 min	2x
Cannellini bean	1 cup	60 min	2x
Chickpeas	1 cup	2-3 hrs	3x
Great Northern beans	1 cup	1-2 hrs	2.5x
Green lentils	1 cup	45 min	2x
Kidney bean	1 cup	60 min	2x

These are some of our favorite combinations but now it's time to put you to the test. Roast, chop, spice, toss, rub, pickle, and play. Let's see what you're made of. Make it grainy. Make it green. Make it great.

CHERRIES, TOMATOES, SHISHITO, BASIL, MINT, WATERMELON, CROUTONS, BALSAMIC, OLIVE OIL, SEA SALT

CUCUMBER, GREEN OLIVES, FETA, TOMATOES, ZUCCHINI, LEAFY GREENS, HERB VINAIGRETTE

ROASTED BROCCOLI, GREENS BEANS, SORREL PESTO, CHILI FLAKES, DUKKAH

ROASTED ASPARAGUS, HERBED CASHEW CREAM

ROASTED FENNEL AND CARROTS, PICKLED RED ONION, HERBS

BARLEY, EGGPLANT, FETA, OLIVES, TAHINI VINAIGRETTE

CHICKPEAS, LEMON, CHILI FLAKES, HERBS, BEETS, PICKLED CABBAGE

COUSCOUS, ROASTED CHERRY TOMATOES, FETA, OLIVES, LEMON, PARSLEY

LACINATO KALE, SWEET POTATO, RED CABBAGE, APPLE, POMEGRANATE, MISO-LEMON VINAIGRETTE.

COUSCOUS, FIGS, RADICCHIO, LEMON, POMEGRANATE SALSA

GREAT NORTHERN BEANS, RADISH, SNAP PEAS, CHOPPED ASPARAGUS, PESTO

CARROT, CABBAGE, RADISH, CUCUMBER, SUNFLOWER SEEDS, ARUGULA, STOCK VINAIGRETTE

BARLEY, PAPRIKA, WINTER SQUASH, KALE, POMEGRANATE, PARSLEY, TAHINI VINAIGRETTE

SPICED CHICKPEAS, TURMERIC PICKLED FENNEL, BLOOD ORANGE, BITTER GREENS

PESTO RUBBED FARRO, WILD MUSHROOMS, WINTER SQUASH, PICKLED RAISINS, DILL

But before we know, we ask.

What would you like?

It can be such fun to know. The answer, a secret, a language.

Martini please!

To whom do we toast?

To you!

Where are you from?

New Jersey

4:00 PM

Can we sit for a drink?

Yes you can!

Are you still serving food? Dinner is at 5.

At 4PM, the question of the hour is:

Drinks are poured, appetites grow, and minds wander to wonder…

THE DIMES MOTHER SAUCES

A good sauce or dressing can instantly transform your experience from simply satiating to transcendent. Sauces are such an important component to impart flavor, color, and texture into your food. They are also a great way to make use for all of those Velveteen herbs and veggies that still have tons of life left in them. Sauces are great receptors for creativity and playfulness in the kitchen — We've created some of our favorite recipes through experiments, mistakes, and follies. Cooking is an extension of personality and mood after all — your emotions infusing all that you put on the table. While there are some rules that are there for good reason (read: emulsions) it's important to leave room for the freedom of discovery, the beauty of the unexpected, and the celebration of curiosity.

At Dimes, you'll find our sauces massaged into grains and pasta, spooned over fish, stirred into soup, spread on sandwiches, and used as dips. We use them everywhere with no judgement while proudly flouting the rules. We employ fearless experimentation and exploration and we encourage it in you.

CURTIDO <3
(Salvadorian Lacto-Fermented Pickles)
Cabbage, radish, carrot, jalapeno,
garlic, salt, cumin, coriander
Made at Dimes 143 Division St NYC
DIMES
DIMES
HOUSE VINAIGRETTE
DIMES
HOUSE
DRESSING
$7.00

Pesto is one of those things that can be seen as a little basic but lends itself to a ton of different applications. It's a super easy way to elevate a simple meal into something a bit more special. You should always have some in your fridge. Pesto works well as a classic pasta sauce or massaged into some grains for a grain bowl. You can also use it as a condiment for fish and meats, or as a sandwich spread. This recipe can be adjusted in unlimited ways. It's a lot of fun to play around with and easy to put together with whatever ingredients you have in your fridge. If you don't have kale use arugula, chard, sorrel, or another leafy green you like. Sub mint for basil. Use sunflower seeds instead of almonds to make it nut free, or use another type of nut. It's a great way to extend the life of any items in your fridge that are about to start wilting. It also works as a sneaky way to trick kids into eating vegetables (and probably would work well on veggie-phobic adults that need some more iron too)!

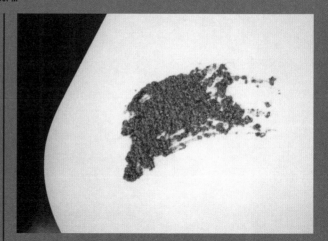

KALE-ALMOND PESTO

PUT ON EVERYTHING AND DON'T APOLOGIZE

MAKES 2 CUPS

1 cup kale, any kind will do, stems removed and roughly chopped
1 cup basil leaves
½ cup parsley leaves
Scant ½ cup sliced toasted almonds

2 garlic cloves
½ cup olive oil, plus more if needed to consistency
¼ cup lemon juice
1 ½ tsps salt

Put all ingredients in the food processor and blend to a loose, chunky consistency. Taste and add more lemon juice and salt if needed until bright and delicious.

BEST PRACTICES

If you don't have almonds, use walnuts, cashews, or pretty much any other nut. If nuts make your body mad use sunflower or pumpkin seeds.

Be free with leaves and herbs. If you just can't with kale, use arugula for a peppery pesto or sorrel for a super bright and lemony one. Swap out parsley for mint. Or basil for dill. Or cilantro for basil. Play musical chairs with your soft herbs. Don't be so uptight.

Lime juice instead of lemon juice is also fun. Add red chili flakes for heat.

CILANTRO SALSA VERDE

THAT FEELING THAT SOMETHING'S MISSING?
THIS IS THE SOLUTION:
COMPLETE YOUR MEAT, FISH, AND POTATOES

MAKES 2 CUPS

1 jalapeno
1 tbsp dijon mustard
2 tbsps honey
1 cup toasted pepita
1 garlic clove
¼ cup plus 2 tbsps
   lime juice
¼ cup orange juice

2 tbsps white
   wine vinegar
3 cups cilantro, packed
1 cup parsley, packed
2 tbsps olive oil plus more
   for desired consistency
2 tsps salt

Put all ingredients in the food processor and blend to
a loose, chunky consistency. Add more oil if needed
to achieve desired body.

MANGO SALSA

GO MANGO OR GO HOME
REGULAR SALSAS' SASSY KID SISTER

MAKES 2 CUPS

1 mango, diced
¼ red onion, diced
1 red thai chili, minced
½ jalapeno, minced
¼ cup cilantro,
   finely chopped
¼ cup tomato, diced

½ cucumber, diced
2 garlic cloves, minced
2 tbsps white wine vinegar
2 tbsps lime juice
2 tsps salt
1 tsp black pepper

Mix all ingredients. Taste and adjust seasonings.

BUT MANGOES MAKE MY MOUTH ITCH...

So use pineapples. Or pomegranate seeds. Forget the
sweet stuff entirely and use more tomato for a classic
salsa experience. If you can't find thai chili, use extra
jalapeno or stir in some red chili flakes to desired
level of heat. If you think cilantro tastes like soap, use
parsley or mint. Apple cider vinegar or rice vinegar
would be nice too.

Time saver (or for you smooth peanut butter people):
rough chop everything and pulse it in your food
processor for a loose and dip-able salsa. Put it on
whatever you want. We like it on our eggs.

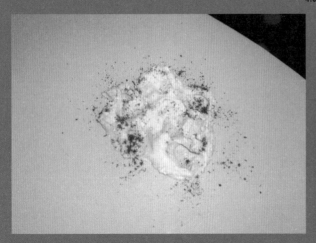

HUMMUS

THE EASIEST THING IN THE WORLD TO MAKE AT HOME THAT NO ONE MAKES AT HOME

MAKES 2 CUPS

½ cup dry chickpeas
    (or 1 ½ cups canned —
    no judgement)
½ tsp baking soda
    (omit if using canned)
1 garlic clove

½ tbsp tahini
1 ½ tsps salt, divided
½ cup olive oil plus more if
    needed to consistency
2 tbsps lemon juice

If using canned chickpeas, skip to the second paragraph. Soak dried chickpeas and baking soda in cold water overnight. Cover with at least triple the amount of water to chickpeas. Drain and rinse chickpeas and transfer to a large pot. Cover with cold water, again, about triple the amount of water to chickpeas, and add 1 ½ teaspoons salt. Bring to a boil and reduce heat, simmering for about 2 hours or until very soft. Strain through a sieve, set aside, and let cool completely.

Place chickpeas, garlic, tahini, salt, olive oil, and lemon juice in the bowl of a food processor. Process until very, very smooth adding more olive oil if needed to create a creamy texture. Taste and add more salt and lemon juice if needed.

FREESTYLES

Following the basic recipe, get wild with any of the following:

Green hummus: throw in any soft herb leaves (basil, parsley, mint, cilantro...)

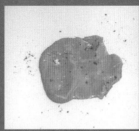

Spicy hummus: add in a spoonful of harissa, or red chili flakes, or anything else to make it hot. If using whole peppers, roughly chop first before adding in.

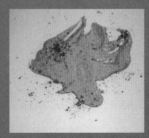

Roasted veggie hummus: throw in some leftover roasted chopped carrots or beets.

Babaghanoush: leave out the chickpeas and olive oil, use 3 cups roasted eggplant instead, add some parsley and voila.

An original Dimes classic, this sauce has been on our tables since day one. Our chef created the recipe in a middle-of-the-night burst of insomniac inspiration just before we opened our first location. Unsure of how it would be received (was it late night genius or sleep deprived insanity?) it turned out the perfect blend of hot, sweet and tangy went well on pretty much any dish. For years, customers would ask us when we were going to start bottling it. It only took us four years to get there, but better late than never. There used to be a green version too but sadly, it was voted off the island.

DIMES HOT SAUCE

SO GOOD WE HAD TO SHARE IT WITH YOU.
IF YOU LOVE SOMETHING, SET IT FREE.

MAKES ABOUT 4 CUPS

18 oz fire roasted red peppers, fresh (DIY) or use high quality jarred

⅛ tsp ghost chili powder (or cayenne)

2 cloves garlic

½ cup mango

½ cup orange juice, freshly squeezed

½ cup white wine vinegar

½ cup brown sugar

¼ cup lime juice, freshly squeezed

½ tbsp salt

Put in a blender and blend. Until very smooth.

MAITAKE RELISH

MAITAKE, YOUR-TAHKI, GIVE YOUR MEATS AND
GRAINS THE RESPECT THEY DESERVE

MAKES ABOUT 1 CUP

- 2 cups maitake mushrooms, chopped into bite-sized pieces
- 2 tbsps olive oil
- ¼ cup pomegranate molasses
- ¼ cup apple cider vinegar
- 1 tbsp lemon juice
- 1 shallot

- 1 tbsp pickled mustard seeds (optional, but encouraged)
- 1 tsp salt plus more for roasting
- 1 tsp aleppo
- ⅛ cup chopped mint
- ⅛ cup chopped parsley
- ½ tsp garlic powder

Preheat oven to 425 °F.

Toss mushrooms with olive oil and spread on a rimmed baking sheet. Roast until brown and crispy. Let cool.

Place remainder of ingredients in mixing bowl. Whisk well, add mushrooms and stir to cover. Store for up to 3 weeks.

RAW BEET CHUTNEY

OOH BABY WE LIKE IT RAW,
SO DO SANDWICHES, MEATS, AND FISH

MAKES 2 CUPS

- 5 oz red beets, peeled and roughly chopped
- 5 oz apples, peeled, cored, and roughly chopped
- 1 garlic clove
- 1 tsp pomegranate molasses
- 1 tsp lime juice

- 2 tsps salt
- ½ cup turmeric ginger concentrate (p 131)
- ½ tsp kashmiri chili powder (or ½ tsp paprika and a pinch cayenne)
- ½ tsp fennel seeds, ground and toasted

Place all ingredients in the bowl of a food processor and process until the consistency of relish — a little chunky.

If you don't have beets or apple, this recipe works great with carrots and citrus.

TURMERIC CASHEW CREAM

ANTI-INFLAMMATORY, ANTI-OXIDANT, ANTI-ESTABLISHMENT, THIS VEGAN ALTERNATIVE WILL RALLY YOUR STATUS QUO VEGGIES AND SOUPS WHEN USED IN PLACE OF YOGURT OR SOFT CHEESE

MAKES 2 ½ CUPS

2 cups cashews, soaked overnight, rinsed with cold water, and drained
2 tbsps ground turmeric
½ cup freshly squeezed lime juice
2 tbsps apple cider vinegar
¾ cup water
½ tbsp salt
1 clove garlic

Put all ingredients in blender and blend until very creamy adding more water if necessary to reach ultimate smoothness.

VARIATIONS

HERBED: Leave out turmeric. Add 3 cups of loose soft herbs such as basil, mint, parsley, and sorrel in any combination.

SPICY: Keep or leave out turmeric and add in a spoonful of harissa, red chili flakes, or anything else to make it hot. If using whole peppers, roughly chop first before adding in.

Sub lemon juice for lime if it suits.

STOCK VINAIGRETTE

GET UP IT'S TIME TO GET DRESSED!!
YOUR SALAD WANTS ITS CINDERELLA MOMENT

MAKES 1 CUP

1 shallot
1 garlic clove
½ tbsp dijon mustard
¼ cup lemon juice
½ tsp salt
¼ cup white wine vinegar
½ cup high quality neutral oil
½ cup extra virgin olive oil

Place all ingredients except oil in a blender and blend until smooth. With the motor running, add oil in a very, very slow and steady stream to emulsify. Take. Your. Time. Once you've nailed this basic dressing, it has endless possibilities for each and every mood swing.

ADD ANY OF THESE DURING STEP 1.

HERB: throw in about a ½ cup of any herb
TAHINI: add ¼ cup
LAVENDER PISTACHIO: add 1 tbsp lavender and ¼ cup pistachio
MISO-LEMON: Add additional ½ cup lemon juice and 2 tbsps white miso paste
TURMERIC GINGER: add 1 tbsp minced ginger and 1 tbsps ground turmeric
CREAMY: add 2-3 tbsps herbed cashew cream for a vegan twist on ranch

BASIC PICKLING LIQUID
WHEN YOU HAVE THAT NOT SO FRESH FEELING,
GIVE IN TO THE SOUR SIDE

MAKES 4 CUPS

2 cups apple cider
   vinegar (or white
   wine vinegar)
2 cups water
½ cup sugar
¼ cup kosher salt
¼ cup garlic cloves,
   smashed

2 bay leaves
1 tbsp pickling spice
   (equal parts coriander
   seed, mustard seed,
   cloves, black pepper-
   corns, whole allspice,
   and red chili flakes)

Place all ingredients in a small stockpot. Bring
to a boil. Pour over vegetables of choice.

CUSTOMIZE

Add in a sliced jalapeno or crushed whole dried
guajillo or ancho chilies for heat.

Double the sugar for a sweeter pickle.

Add a few stems of woody herbs (rosemary, thyme)
for more depth of flavor.

Add 4-5 stems of fresh dill for dill pickles.

Add a tablespoon turmeric for a golden pickle
(my favorite for leftover fennel).

THINGS TO PICKLE

Pickle any leftover veggies from your other projects.
Our favorites: fennel, carrots, cucumber, cabbage,
onions (especially red), beets, peppers (especially
cherry peppers!) — it's literally endless.

MUSTARD SEEDS: one of my favorite pantry items
is pickled mustard seeds. They add instant texture
and acidity to salads, meats, and grains.

RAISINS: especially with the jalapeno pickling liquid.
A great topping for salads and roasted veggies.

CHILIES: especially jalapeno and fresno.

SALMON: let your pickling liquid cool to 100°F or less.
Pour over salmon fillets. Add in some sliced red
onion and dill. Let sit in the liquid for at least 72 hours.
Slice and enjoy.

Keep a double batch of pickling liquid and a big batch
of pickling spice on hand for quick and easy pickling
at any time.

Ghee can be used in place of cooking oil or butter for sautéing and roasting vegetables and proteins. It's a great oil for toasting your grains before boiling, or tossed in as a seasoning for your hot grains and legumes. It has a higher smoke point than many other cooking oils making it a much healthier choice. A higher smoke point means that it is more stable, thus helping to keep phytonutrients intact and reducing the risk of creating harmful free radicals.

O.M.F. GHEE

GHEE YOUR MIND AND THE REST WILL FOLLOW

MAKES ABOUT 1½ CUPS

1 pound organic grass fed butter	1 tsp fennel seeds
	1 tsp whole allspice
1 shallot, chopped	1 whole clove
1 garlic clove, chopped	1 tsp turmeric
1 tsp ginger, chopped	1 cinnamon stick
1 tsp cumin seeds	2 whole cardamom pods
1 tsp coriander seeds	

Slowly melt the butter over medium heat in a small saucepan. When the butter comes to a boil, reduce the heat to very low and simmer, uncovered and undisturbed, about 15-20 minutes.

The butter's water content will foam and make tiny, sharp crackling noises. Watch out for splatter. The ghee is ready when the crackling stops and the sound becomes a rounder, gentler simmer. The butter will turn clear golden and the white sediment will be light tan.

Remove from heat immediately. Let cool slightly and strain through a mesh strainer. Discard spices. Pour into a jar and let cool completely. Store at room temperature for up to 2 months.

NOTE: If you want a neutral ghee to cook with, just leave out everything but the butter and follow the same recipe.

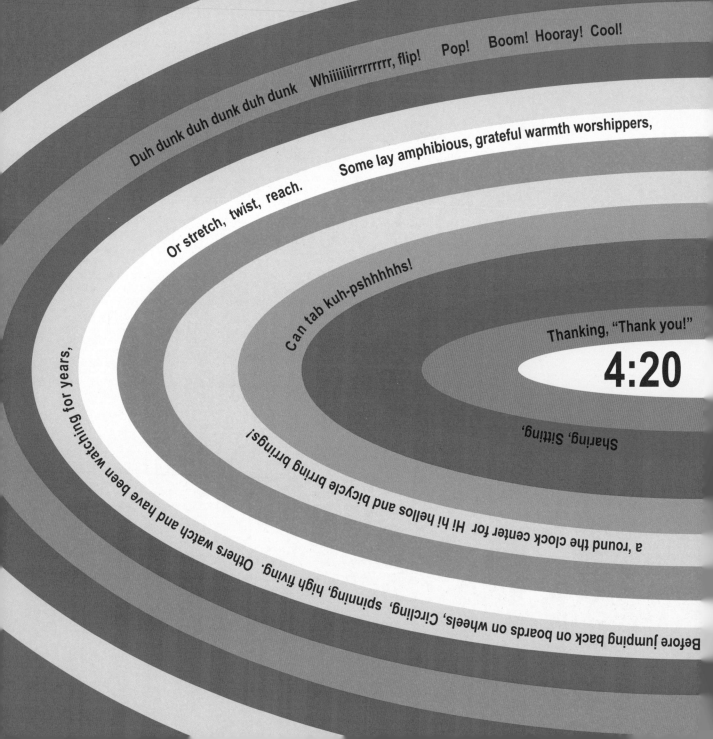

Duh dunk duh dunk duh dunk   Whiiiiiirrrrrrrrr, flip!   Pop!   Boom! Hooray! Cool!

Some lay amphibious, grateful warmth worshippers,

Or stretch, twist, reach.

Can tab kuh-pshhhhhs!

Thanking, "Thank you!"

4:20

Sharing, Sitting,

a 'round the clock center for Hi! hi hellos and bicycle bring brrings!

Before jumping back on boards on wheels, Circling, spinning, high fiving. Others watch and have been watching for years,

Do it again!

....Duh dunk duh dunk duh dunk...

Ages of all kinds make concentric circles in Dimes Square: The age of discovery. The romantic age, Space age, Internet age, Stoned age.

And ah, at 4:20 PM, the golden age. Or at least a golden hour. The sun lowers on the smallest megalith, Dimes henge, a wonder of mysterious origin — whose is it?

Foily unwrappings of burrito chomp chomps!

On a henge of blue stones, some rest for a moment, palms on knees, Hee hoo, hee hoo,

Beneath the lowering sun, it's everyone's —

Iced coffee slurps! Lighter flick flicks!

PM

Dimes Market is close,

Let's take a walk,

Where would you like to go?

To Mexico for a crunchy blue chip?

Is it warm where you go?

Italia! Olio!

New Jersey — what exit?

Hold a tin of homemade hummus,

feel the peanut butter cookie give beneath your thumbs.

----- but what's inside might take you away.

----- Japan, for tea? ----- Matcha or genmaicha?

----- A sweet, ripe tomato. ----- Would you like to go home?

I know, New York is the worst in the winter. It's nothing like your beloved Southern California. Trudging through dirty snowdrifts, darkness creeping in as you realize you're just another pair of anonymous eyes floating in a sea of wool and down. It's hard to be so far from friends and family but no need to be all *Lost in Translation* about it. Admit it, it was pretty amazing when you ate it on black ice in your white coat and cute shoes. Just embrace the boots and long underwear already. It will be summer again soon and those homesick boo-hoos will be toast. Now go microwave a s'more and pretend you're at summer camp.

Food often acts as a time machine, transporting us to childhood and beyond through taste, texture and smell. It can heal, comfort, and anchor us in moments when we feel lost or lonely and are aching for the familiar. Here we embrace that familiarity — those traditions that continue through all of the phases of our lives. The meal your mom makes when you come home for a visit. The meal you crave when you're far from home.

HOMESICK

Angelica Kitchen was a vegetarian icon that pioneered and paved the way for the omnipresent wellness-focused food uprising we are seeing now. Its shuttering after 40 plus years was a true loss and an unfortunate side effect of the ever changing landscape of today's New York. Many, many members of the local community are saddened by the loss. As an homage, we developed our own Dimesy version of their classic cornbread. We make ours with black rice and and a healthy dollop of apple miso butter. How will you make yours?

CORNBREAD

MAKES ONE LOAF

4 cups cooked black rice	½ tbsp sea salt
3 ½ cups apple cider	¼ cup olive or coconut oil
1 ½ cups blue cornmeal	1 ½ tbsps black
⅓ cup chia seeds	sesame seeds

Blend about half of the black rice and apple cider in a blender until smooth then place in a mixing bowl along with remaining ingredients except sesame seeds.

Oil the pan with cooking spray or a little olive oil and sprinkle the bottom with sesame seeds. Pour in the batter and tap on the counter a couple of times to distribute the batter evenly.

Cook at 350 °F for about an hour or until cooked through. A toothpick inserted in the center will come out clean. Serve slathered with miso apple butter.

MISO APPLE BUTTER

MAKES 2 CUPS

3 apples, peeled, cored, and chopped	2 tbsps miso
1 sprig rosemary	⅛ tsp ground allspice
2 tbsps apple cider	¾ tsp cinnamon

Place apples in a small saucepan with rosemary and apple cider. Cook covered over low heat until apples are very, very soft. Remove rosemary and transfer apples to your blender along with miso, allspice, and cinnamon. Purée until very smooth.

DIMES CHILI

SERVES 4

2 tbsps olive oil	1 can Great Northern
1 onion, diced small	beans (15½ oz)
6 garlic cloves, sliced thin	1 can red kidney beans
4 arbol chilies, crushed	(15½ oz)
1 tsp cumin	1 can black beans
½ tsp nutmeg	(15½ oz)
½ tsp cinnamon	1 can whole peeled
2 tsps ground cinnamon	tomatoes (28 oz)
2 tsps ground coriander	3 limes, juice only
1 tsp cardamom	2 tsps salt
2 tsps unsweetened	Fresh black pepper,
cocoa powder	a few cracks
1 tsp paprika	1 head lacinato kale,
¼ tsp cayenne pepper	chopped and wilted
½ tube tomato paste	
1 can crushed	
tomatoes (28 oz)	

Heat olive oil in a medium stock pot. Add onions and garlic and caramelize until lightly browned. Add spices and toast until fragrant. Stir in tomato paste, crushed tomatoes, and beans. Add whole tomatoes and their juices, breaking them apart into small pieces as you add them to the pot. Stir in lime juice, salt, and pepper and cook until thick and flavorful.

Stir in kale and cook until just wilted. Enjoy with Greek yogurt, avocado, and lime wedges.

CURRY

SERVES 2

2 cups eggplant (about half of one), cut into ½ inch pieces	2 inch piece of ginger, peeled and minced
1 yellow bell pepper, stem and seeds removed, cut into ½ inch strips	3 tbsps curry paste (red or green)
1 zucchini, or any summer squash, cut into ½ inch dice	1 can coconut milk (13.5 oz)
	½ cup water
	3 lime leaves
1 head broccoli, chopped into bite-sized pieces	2 tbsps lime juice
	1 tsp fish sauce (vegans: sub liquid aminos)
2 tbsp coconut oil	½ cup cilantro, divided; stems finely chopped, whole leaves reserved for garnish
1 small yellow onion, thinly sliced	
3 garlic cloves, thinly sliced	1 tsp salt

Toss each of the vegetables separately in olive oil to lightly coat and season with a little salt. Roast at 400 until light golden brown and tender and set aside. To save oven space, eggplant and zucchini can be combined on one tray and peppers and broccoli on the other.

Saute onion, garlic, and ginger in coconut oil over medium heat until translucent. Add curry paste and toast for a couple of minutes. Stir in coconut milk, water, lime leaves and juice, fish sauce, cilantro stems, and salt. Simmer for 10 minutes.

Add vegetables and cook until heated through. Serve over rice, quinoa, broccoli rice, or any other grain. Garnish with whole cilantro leaves.

ADD A PROTEIN FOR HEFT

Tofu, shrimp, diced chicken, or diced beef. Raw proteins can be added while the sauce is simmering. Continue to cook until protein is cooked all the way through then stir in vegetables.

ALBERTO'S POZOLE

SERVES 4-6

BASE

1 can hominy (30 oz), drained and rinsed well	1 oregano stem
2 quarts of water	2 garlic cloves, minced
½ white onion, diced	4 tsps salt
1 jalapeno pepper finely chopped	2 whole chicken breasts (about 10 oz), cut into ½ inch dice
1 bay leaf	

OREGANO SAUCE

4 tomatillos, roughly chopped	½ cup fresh oregano leaves
1 garlic clove	2 tbsps yuzu juice (or fresh lime juice)
1 green thai chili	1 tsp salt
½ cup of olive oil	½ tsp black pepper
½ cup cilantro leaves	

MAKE POZOLE BASE: Put hominy, water, onion, jalapeno, bay leaf, oregano, garlic, and salt in a large pot. Bring to a boil and simmer for 15-20 minutes.

Add chicken breast and cook until done, about 5 minutes. Set aside.

MAKE OREGANO SAUCE: Purée all sauce ingredients in a blender until very smooth. Mix sauce into pozole (about 4 tablespoons per cup, or more to taste) just before serving or color will brown.

We serve ours with sautéed plantains (sliced and quartered) and garnish with watercress and radish but feel free to use whatever greens and crunchy veggies you have on hand.

MOQUECA
BRAZILIAN FISH STEW

SERVES 4-6

2   limes juiced
¼ cup olive oil
½ tsp red pepper flakes
4   garlic cloves
    chopped, divided
2   tsps salt, divided
18 large shrimp (about
    1 lb) cleaned and peeled
3   pounds cod fillet
    cut into 2 inch pieces
1   large yellow onion
    chopped

5   plum tomatoes chopped
2   green bell peppers
    chopped
8   leaves of hearty greens
    destemmed and thinly
    chopped (kale, chard,
    collards)
1   cup finely chopped
    cilantro + parsley leaves
1   cup canned
    coconut milk

Mix lime juice, olive oil, red pepper flakes, 1/2 chopped garlic, and 1 1/2 teaspoons salt in a medium bowl. Add the fish and toss to coat. Cover with cling film and place in the fridge to marinate for 30 minutes to an hour.

Layer each ingredient like sand art in a heavy pot starting from the bottom: onion, tomatoes, bell peppers, greens, remaining ½ teaspoon salt, cod, cilantro, and parsley. Arrange shrimp on the top layer over herbs. Pour remaining marinade liquid and coconut milk over shrimp.

Over medium high heat, bring to a boil, then cover the pot and adjust heat to gently simmer until vegetables are soft and fish is cooked, about 20 minutes. Serve with rice and any extra fresh herbs.

SHEPHERD'S PIE

SERVES 4-6

3 lbs potatoes peeled and cut into 1 inch dice
1 cup whole milk
½ cup butter
2 lbs ground lamb or beef
3 tbsps olive oil
1 large yellow onion, finely chopped
3 garlic cloves, minced
1 small fennel bulb, finely chopped
1 small head celery root, finely chopped
1 large carrot, finely chopped
1 large parsnip, finely chopped

1 bunch swiss chard, chopped into bite-sized pieces
2 tbsps tomato paste
1 tbsp all purpose flour
1 cup dry red wine
2 cups chicken or beef stock
1 tbsp Worcestershire
3 tsps salt, divided
1 tbsp rosemary, finely chopped
1 tbsp thyme leaves, finely chopped
1 tbsp sage, finely chopped
Fresh black pepper

Place potatoes in a large stockpot covered by cold salted water. Simmer until very soft. Drain potatoes well through a mesh sieve and place back in the stockpot. Make mashed potatoes: add milk, butter, and 1 teaspoon salt and mash with a hand masher until combined, adding more milk if necessary to consistency. Set aside.

Heat a large deep skillet or stockpot to medium high heat and cook meat in batches until nicely browned. Transfer to a bowl with a slotted spoon to drain off extra fat.

Drain off any leftover fat but do not clean the pan. Add olive oil and heat over medium-high heat. Add vegetables and cook until lightly browned. Add tomato paste and flour and cook stirring constantly until paste darkens, about 1 minute.

Add wine, bring to a simmer and cook until reduced by half. Add stock, Worcestershire, remaining 2 teaspoons salt, and herbs. Return meat to the pan and simmer, stirring occasionally until liquid is evaporated and sauce is thickened.

Transfer to a deep 3-quart casserole dish and, using a rubber spatula, spread top carefully with the mashed potatoes so that the filling is completely covered. Season with a few cracks of black pepper.

Bake until the filling bubbles around the edges and potatoes are golden brown. For crispier potatoes, flash under the broiler for 1-2 minutes before serving.

VEGAN MAC + CHEESE WITH SHIITAKE BACON

SERVES 4-6

4 cups shiitake mushrooms, stems removed and thinly sliced
2 tsps paprika
½ lb winter squash (such as blue hubbard, kabocha, or butternut), peeled, seeds removed, and diced into large chunks
1 yellow onion, thinly sliced
2 garlic cloves, thinly sliced
5 sage leaves
½ lb broccoli, chopped into bite-sized pieces
1 lb pasta (such as campanelle, shells, anything with nooks + crannies)
½ block silken tofu
2 tbsps rice vinegar
½ cup plus 4 tbsps olive oil, divided
3 tsps salt, divided

Place mushrooms in a medium mixing bowl. Toss with paprika, 2 teaspoons salt, and 2 tablespoons olive oil. Roast at 400 °F until crispy, stirring occasionally.

Toss squash with 2 tablespoons olive oil. Roast at 375 °F until very tender.

Meanwhile, caramelize onions, garlic, sage, and remaining half cup of olive oil in a large skillet over high heat. Transfer to a bowl and set aside.

Use the same skillet to sauté the broccoli, add more oil if needed to lightly coat. Saute over medium-high heat until just tender.

Boil a large stockpot of water and cook pasta according to packaging. Drain pasta and place back in stockpot.

Place roasted squash, caramelized onion mixture, tofu, rice vinegar, and remaining 2 teaspoons of salt in a blender and blend until very smooth and creamy. Add sauce to the stockpot and stir to combine. Fold in broccoli and shiitake bacon.

Enjoy with TONS of hot sauce. We particularly like ours with Crystal Hot Sauce or Frank's Red Hot.

WINTER VEG + WHITE BEAN CASSEROLE

SERVES 6-8

¾ cup ghee, divided
1 large onion, thinly sliced
6 garlic cloves, thinly sliced
2 tbsps ginger, minced
¼ cup chopped sage
4 cups vegetable stock
1 cup kale almond pesto (p 90)
1 tbsp smoked paprika
1 tbsp sumac
1 tbsp apple cider vinegar
1 tbsp lemon juice
2 tbsps white miso
1 tsp salt
2 tbsps rolled oats

2 cups cooked white beans (such as Great Northern or cannelini)
1 delicata (or other winter squash) cut into half moons
1 head of cauliflower, cut into bite-sized florets
1 medium sweet potato, peeled, cut into ½ inch cubes
1 bunch kale, thick stems removed, cut into bite-sized pieces
2 cups breadcrumbs
¾ cup grated Parmesan cheese

Heat ¼ cup ghee in a large pot. Add onion, garlic, ginger, and sage and sauté until translucent.

Add vegetable stock, pesto, smoked paprika, sumac, apple cider vinegar, lemon juice, miso, and salt. Stir together thoroughly and bring to a boil.

Add oats, beans, and vegetables. Reduce heat to a simmer, cover, and cook until sweet potatoes are just tender, about 15-20 minutes. Transfer to a deep casserole dish and set aside.

Heat remaining ½ cup ghee in a large skillet. Add breadcrumbs and coat thoroughly. Cook for a minute or two and remove from heat. Place breadcrumbs in a small bowl and mix with Parmesan. Spread evenly over the top of the casserole.

Bake at 400 °F until deep golden brown and bubbling, about 35 minutes. Place a sheet tray on the shelf below to catch drips.

NOTES:
To make vegan, sub coconut or olive oil for ghee and ½ cup nutritional yeast for parmesan.

To make gluten free, sub gluten free breadcrumbs, quinoa puffs, or crushed puffed rice.

8:00 PM

Back at 8PM, our spherical pairs.

And at Dimes, pairs in chairs exchange lingering stares.

A server sets down two plump scallops.

Half on one fork, half on the other.

Tines entwined, a salty, "cheers!"

How lovely when a couple shares.

A couple of lovers, a couple of friends.

Are they talking, are they dancing?

Excitement softens the difference.

Imagine a magnet on each person's nose,

drawing them in, Drawing a heart.

Thighs lift from seats,

elbows inch closer to those across the table,

To hear, to say,   To touch.

Why?   It's magnetic!   It's electric!

It's six weeks in. You're ecstatic, thrilled, smiling from ear to ear. It doesn't even bother you that he has four roommates. And isn't it so awesome that he can remain close with his ex? You spent all day grocery shopping. You went to Dimes Market, Union Square, and Kalustyan's to get everything you need to make the PERFECT meal. The food is local, organic, gluten-free, dairy-free ("we're allergic!") hand-picked, and solar-powered. The wine is biodynamic, made by women, orange, and unpronounceable. The table is set just right—it doesn't matter that it's your coffee table. This is going to be the best night...

HONEY

MOON

These are the meals you make when you can take your time, setting the scene, everything just so. Meals you have time to luxuriate over (or that looked like you did), meals you make when you want to impress. Even if your dating style is more *Her* than *Lady and the Tramp* you've still gotta eat, right? And if it doesn't work out, there's always more fish in the sea.

This is your show-off food. This is confidence. This is beauty. This is the *honeymoon.*

HANDY DANDY FISH CHART

Hello. We like you a lot. So we're trying to make life a little easier for you by taking out some of the guess-work. You've got a life to live, dates to plan, people to romance. Fish can be tricky — there are so many types! Just like people. If only you could tell a good partner by the clarity of their eyes, the firmness of their flesh, the color of their gills. Sigh. If only.

Just like in dating, it's important to treat the bodies of others with the respect they deserve. And, just like in dating, time, patience, and a little finesse can yield beautiful results. While speed, thoughtlessness, and stupidity will leave you in tears. And hungry.

This chart shows you the best cooking methods for a variety of our favorite fish. Cook responsibly.

LEAN	MID-FAT	FATTY
Cod	Arctic char	Mackerel
Flounder	Salmon	Sardines
Haddock	Tilapia	Herring
Sea bass	Tuna	Anchovies
Sole	Trout	Black Cod
POACH / BAKE	SEAR / BROIL / CRUST	SEAR / BROIL

BROIL

This is a quick, easy, and healthful way to prepare fish.

Preheat your broiler on high for about 7-10 minutes. Meanwhile, gently brush or drizzle your fish on both sides and season all over with salt and pepper.

Place your fish, skin side down, on a rimmed baking sheet about 2-4 inches below the flame and broil until fish is opaque and flakes easily.

BROILED SARDINES WITH MEYER LEMON SALSA

SERVES 2

3 meyer lemons (or regular lemons)	1 tbsp sumac
¼ cup pickled red onion	1 tsp red chili flakes
¼ cup parsley, finely chopped	¼ cup apple cider vinegar
¼ cup mint, finely chopped	2 tbsps olive oil
¼ cup dill, finely chopped	1 tsp salt
¼ cup capers	1 lbs sardines, cleaned (DIY or flirt with your fishmonger)

Keeping skin on, slice lemons into very thin rounds. Then slice each round into quarters. Remove any seeds that don't come out during slicing.

Place lemons in a small mixing bowl along with red onion, herbs, capers, sumac, chili flakes, vinegar, olive oil, and salt. Stir to combine and set aside.

Broil sardines according to instructions at left. Top with salsa.

SAUTÉ

Another quick and easy preparation, sautéeing is frying quickly in a little bit of fat. This works best for lean, thin cuts of fish with shorter cooking times. Heat about 2 tablespoons olive oil or butter in a sauté pan. Pat your fish dry with paper towels on both sides and season well with salt and pepper. Cook your fish for a few minutes on the first side, flip with a fish spatula and cook through on the other side. If cooking shrimp (a perfect candidate for this method) flip every couple of minutes to be sure each shrimp cooks evenly.

SHRIMP + FONIO GRITS

Fonio is an ancient grain native to West Africa. A staple food there, it's been uncovered in the tombs of Egyptian pyramids. One of the world's oldest superfoods, it's a rich, gluten-free source of amino acids, fiber, and iron. A bit of a chameleon, it can be cooked like traditional couscous, porridge, polenta, or used in cakes. Here we use it as a fun alternative to traditional hominy grits.

SERVES 3-4

2 tbsps butter
6¾ cups water, divided
1 tbsp miso
2 tbsps nutritional yeast
1 tbsp turmeric
3 tsps salt, divided
1 tsp black pepper, divided
1 cup fonio
2 tbsps olive oil
½ cup sausage or chorizo, out of casing and crumbled

2 garlic cloves, thinly sliced
3 scallions, chopped, divided
¼ tsp red pepper flakes
1 pint heirloom cherry tomatoes
10 medium sized shrimp, cleaned
½ cup cilantro, divided; stems reserved and finely chopped, whole leaves for garnish
1 pinch Aleppo chili

BAKE

Baking is a great technique to impart tons of flavor to lean, delicate fish that can become easily dry and overcooked with direct heat methods. Vegetables take equal billing here, creating a one pot dish that can be enjoyed with your favorite grain for a quick and easy meal. Preheat your oven to 300 °F. Place your fish in the center of your vegetables and cook about 25-30 minutes. Fish will flake easily with a fork when it's ready.

Vegetables that cook in the 15-20 minute range work best here. If you MUST use a root vegetable or hard squash add your casserole dish to the oven without fish and cook for 15-20 minutes on its own or about ¾ of the way cooked. (Refer back to pp 71–74 for our handy vegetable cooking guide). Then add your fish and cook for an additional 25-30 minutes until your fish is done.

Melt butter in a small stockpot. Add 6 cups water, bring to a boil, and whisk in miso until completely incorporated. Whisk in nutritional yeast, turmeric, 1 ½ teaspoons salt, and ½ teaspoon black pepper. Stir in fonio. Lower the heat to a simmer and cook until the the fonio becomes creamy and thickened, stirring frequently, until it becomes the consistency of traditional grits or creamy polenta, about 15 minutes.

Heat olive oil in a large sauté pan. Add sausage and cook, stirring until sausage is nicely browned. Add garlic, half of the scallions, red pepper flakes, and cilantro stems and cook a few minutes until fragrant. Add cherry tomatoes and ¼ cup water and cook, stirring occasionally until tomatoes begin to burst.

Meanwhile, pat shrimp dry. Add to pan along with remaining salt and pepper once tomatoes begin to burst. The liquid will thicken and reduce quickly. Continue to add remaining water, ¼ cup at a time until tomatoes are completely burst and shrimp are pink and cooked through.

Spoon over hot fonio grits and top with cilantro leaf, remaining chopped scallion, and a sprinkle of aleppo chili.

HARISSA ROASTED COD

SERVES 4

1 lb creamer potatoes cut into bite-sized pieces	1 lb skinless cod cut into four pieces
1 fennel bulb cut into ¼ inch wedges	1 cup cilantro leaves

SAUCE

1⅓ cups roasted red peppers	4 tsps harissa
2 garlic cloves	1 tsp salt
1 shallot	6 tbsps lime juice
4 tsps fresh orange juice	4 tsps greek yogurt
4 tsps fresh lemon juice	1 tsp fish sauce
4 tsps orange blossom water	3 tbsps chopped pistachio
4 tsps honey	¼ bunch cilantro, leaves and stems roughly chopped

SALSA

3 blood oranges, skin and pith removed and chopped	1 tsp salt
½ cup pickled red onion	1 tbsp pomegranate molasses
¼ cup lime juice	¼ bunch cilantro, leaves and stems finely chopped

Put potatoes in a small stockpot and cover with salted water by about two inches. Simmer until just tender, drain and set aside.

Meanwhile, make sauce by blending all ingredients in a blender until smooth.

Place tender potatoes into a deep 3-quart casserole dish along with fennel wedges. Add sauce and toss gently to coat.

Season fish all over with salt and pepper and place on top of vegetables about 1-2 inches apart. Drizzle with some good olive oil.

Cover the casserole dish with foil, or with a lid, and bake at 400 °F for 1 hour or until vegetables are very tender.

While the fish is cooking, make salsa by combining all ingredients in a small mixing bowl.

Serve with plenty of blood orange salsa and remaining cup of cilantro leaves.

Toss eggplant, fresno chilies, cherry tomatoes, zucchini, onion, garlic, lemon juice, chopped basil, capers, olive oil and 2 teaspoons salt. Place in a deep 3-quart casserole dish.

Season fish all over with salt and pepper and place on top of vegetables about 1-2 inches apart. Drizzle with some good olive oil and scatter lemon slices on top.

Cover the casserole dish with foil, or with a lid, and bake at 400 °F for 45 minutes or until tomatoes are bursting and the rest is very tender.

Hand tear the remaining basil leaves and scatter on top. Serve with crusty grilled bread (garlic bread would not be a bad choice here).

BAKED SOLE
WITH RATATOUILLE

SERVES 4

1 eggplant, diced into half inch cubes
3 fresno chilies, stems removed and chopped
1 pint cherry tomatoes
1 zucchini, diced into ½ inch cubes
½ yellow onion, thinly sliced
3 garlic cloves, thinly sliced

2 tbsps fresh lemon juice
1 bunch basil leaves, reserve 3 leaves and finely chop the rest
1 tbsp capers, drained
1 cup olive oil
2 tsps salt plus more to taste
1 lb skinless sole
1 lemon, thinly sliced into rounds, seeds removed

POACH

A richly flavored poaching liquid is key here and works best with lean to mid-fat fish profiles. Place your poaching liquid in a high sided skillet. Bring to a boil and reduce heat to a simmer. Let simmer for 10 minutes before adding fish to allow extra time for flavors to harmonize. Meanwhile, season your fish all over with salt and pepper. Add your fish and cook at a very gentle simmer until fish flakes easily with a fork. When the fish is done, gently remove it from the liquid with a fish spatula, or wide metal spatula. Strain the solids out of the liquid and add 2 cups back to the pan. Turn heat to high, and reduce the liquid into a sauce. Or serve your fish with a side of pesto, or simply some good olive oil and fresh lemon juice.

SERVING SUGGESTIONS

Classic Poached Flounder with Great Northern beans, radish, snap peas, chopped asparagus, pesto (p 83).

Thai Poached Cod with black rice and fresh cilantro.

Heirloom Poached Sole with cucumber, green olives, feta, cherry tomatoes, zucchini, leafy greens, herb vinaigrette (p 82).

CLASSIC

SERVES 4

3 ½ cups cold water
½ bottle white wine
½ lemon, cut
  into thin rounds
½ bunch dill
½ bunch parsley

½ tbsp fennel seeds
½ tbsp coriander seeds
½ tsp black peppercorns
1 tbsp salt
4 pieces of fish
  (about 6 oz each)

If reducing to a sauce, add two tablespoons cold butter.

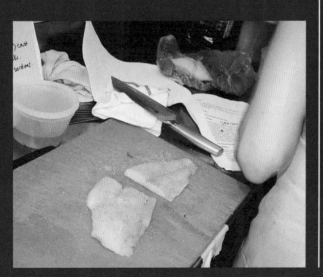

THAI

SERVES 4

3 cups coconut water
3 cups water
¼ cup yellow curry paste (whisk in thoroughly when liquid starts to boil)
2 lime leaves
½ tsp red chili flakes
½ bunch cilantro

1 tsp salt
½ tsp black peppercorn
2 stalks lemongrass chopped into 3 inch pieces and bruised with flat side of knife
4 pieces of fish (about 6 oz each)

The strained liquid works great as a sauce for mussels. Bring strained liquid to a boil, reduce to a simmer, add cleaned mussels, and cook until all mussel shells are opened. Serve mussels in the sauce with crusty bread and lots of fresh cilantro or thai basil.

HEIRLOOM

SERVES 4

1 quart heirloom cherry tomatoes
½ tbsp fennel seeds
Olive oil to coat
3½ cups water
½ bunch basil
1½ tsps salt plus more to taste

1 tsp black pepper
1 garlic clove
¼ cup tomato paste
2 tbsps capers
4 pieces of fish (about 6 oz each)

Toss tomatoes in olive oil to coat. Season with salt to taste. Stir in fennel seeds. Spread tomatoes on a baking sheet. Roast at 400 °F until bursting.

Remove from oven and let cool slightly. Transfer to a blender and blend until smooth with remaining ingredients except fish. Follow poaching directions on left hand page.

This liquid is already pretty thick and doesn't need to be reduced. Makes a great sauce as is without additional work.

SEAR

Searing is a direct, high heat cooking method so it's best reserved for our mid-fat fish friends. This is the trickiest of our fish techniques but we have total faith in you. Here are our tips for the crispiest, crunchiest skin with tender middles.

Preheat your oven to 375 °F. (This step is only necessary if your fish is more than an inch thick.)

Heat your pan. Place an oven proof, non-stick skillet over high heat. Pump that heat all the way up. Let heat for about 2 minutes on high, then add a neutral cooking oil with a high smoke point. (Canola is your friend here).

Dry, Dry, Dry. This word is the first step to crispy skinned fish. While your pan is heating, place the fish on a plate or cutting board. Using a paper towel, pat thoroughly all over to remove as much surface moisture as possible. Do not do this step ahead of time!! Moisture will rise back up the longer it sits.

Salt your fish on all sides. Do not do this ahead of time — salt draws out moisture and is the enemy of good browning. Season with a few cracks of fresh black pepper too.

When your oil is very hot but not smoking, add the fish to the pan skin side down. Do not overcrowd your pan. There should be around two inches between each piece of fish. If the pan is too full, the fish will steam and you will have soggy skin. GROSS. Press the fish into the pan to make sure the entire piece of skin is getting good contact with your pan. Now don't touch it. Seriously. Leave it alone for a long time. 5-8 minutes or so until it's VERY browned and crispy. The majority of your total cooking time is happening skin side down. Once the skin is looking gorgeous, flip it. If it's a thick piece of fish, transfer to the oven to finish cooking for another 8 minutes or so. If it's a thin piece of fish, cook for 2-3 minutes more in the pan after flipping.

CRUST

A super easy way to impress is to dress your fish up with a crust. If you choose to go this way, use skinless fish in the mid-fat family. Salmon and tuna are your best bets.

THREE CRUSTS THAT WON'T DISAPPOINT:

SESAME: black, white or a combination of both makes a nutty and crunchy crust.

ZA'ATAR: this Middle Eastern spice blend is bright and herbaceous.

FURIKAKE: this Japanese condiment imparts citrusy umami notes. Buy pre-made or make at home with our recipe on the opposite page.

Preheat oven to 400 degrees.

Pour a ½ cup of your crust of choice onto a plate. Season your fish all over with salt and coat the fish with seeds on all sides.

Heat 2 tablespoons olive oil in an oven-proof non-stick skillet until very hot but not smoking.

Add the fish to the pan and cook until the seeds are golden brown on one side. Flip the fish over and transfer the pan to the oven.

Cook for another 8-12 minutes depending on the thickness of the fish. To check for doneness, gently break open the underside.

HOMEMADE FURIKAKE

MAKES ABOUT 1 CUP

¼ cup orange zest
4 sheets nori
½ cup packed bonito flakes
6 tbsps toasted white or
  black sesame seeds

2 tsps black salt (or pink
  or kosher salt)
2 tsps high quality sugar

Spread orange zest on a baking sheet and dry out
in a 200 °F oven, about 5 minutes. Don't let it brown.
Remove and let cool.

Grind nori and bonito in a blender or spice grinder.
Place in a bowl with sesame, dried orange zest, black
salt, and sugar in a bowl and mix together.

Place in a jar with a tight fitting lid and use for up to
2 months.

IDEAS

**Sesame Crusted Salmon + Miso Quinoa Risotto
with Butternut, Shiitake and Sage (p 79)**

Za'atar Crusted Tuna with Freekeh Pilaf (p 76)

**Furikake Crusted Char over carrot, red cabbage,
radish, cucumber, sunflower seeds, arugula,
stock vinaigrette (p 83)**

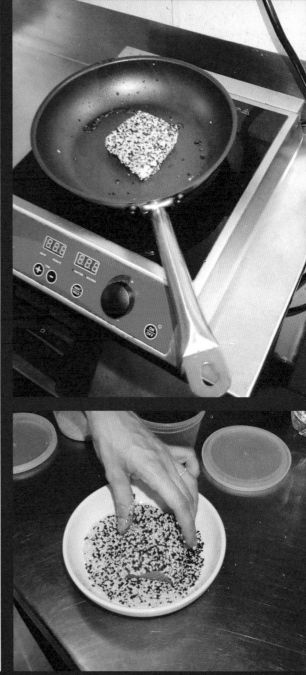

The people are wearing masks, but no one is hiding anything. Cheshire cat grins. Tragedy mask frowns. Open-mouthed Ohs and closed-eyed my Gods. At 10PM Dimes is an operatic cocktail of they did shaken with they didn't, I will stirred with you won't, And a little "Can you believe it?!" shaved on top

10:00

New York is a spectacular place for all kinds of commiserating. A night out can be nothing more complicated than posting up on the big rock in the triangle outside of Dimes where friends appear as if by telepathy to talk and hang late into the evening. Other times the bar is boss and cocktails flow like tears.

Any way you play it, there's almost always a drink in hand. Here are some of our favorites to make at home on those nights you can't make it through the door.

Oh, and don't forget the chocolate.

WHEATGRASS MARGARITA

MAKES 1 PERFECT MARGARITA, DOUBLE THE RECIPE IF SOCIAL

2 oz wheatgrass tequila	½ oz simple syrup
1 oz dolin blanc	1 little old slice of beet
¾ oz lime	

Shake all ingredients except beet with ice and strain in 10oz cocktail glass over ice. Garnish with beet slice.

WHEATGRASS TEQUILA

Handful of fresh wheatgrass	1 bottle tequila (750ml)

Blend tequila and wheatgrass switching from low to high over a good amount of time. Strain and squeeze to extract all liquid. Return to tequila bottle and store in fridge.

SIMPLE SYRUP

Mix together:
1 cup sugar
1 ½ cups boiling water

MILK RIVER

MAKES 1, DOUBLE THE RECIPE, YOU'RE GOING TO WANT AN ENCORE

3 oz nigori sake	Pinch of ginger
½ oz lemon juice	powder and crushed
½ oz simple syrup	fennel seeds
Lemon zest	

Shake all ingredients except zest with ice and strain in 10oz glass over fresh ice. Garnish with lemon zest and float down the river.

LOVING LOVE

MAKES 1, DOUBLE THE RECIPE TO INCLUDE LOVED ONES

1.5 oz rum	A crack of fresh
½ oz Ancho Reyes Chili Liqueur	black pepper
½ oz lime juice	A couple of edible flowers
1 oz turmeric ginger concentrate	

Shake all ingredients except pepper and flowers with ice and strain in a cocktail glass over fresh ice. Garnish with ground pepper + flower. Love that love.

TURMERIC GINGER CONCENTRATE

MAKES 2 CUPS (OR 16 COCKTAIL PORTIONS) USE ANY EXTRA IN YOUR BEET CHUTNEY (P 94)

1 tsp black pepper	1 ½ cups water
5 oz ginger, peeled and chopped	1 ½ oz lime juice
1 oz turmeric , same as ginger	1 ½ oz agave

Blend all ingredients and strain.

UME SHISO SELTZER

MAKES 16 PORTIONS

4 oz umeboshi paste	¼ cup coconut sugar
1 oz lemon juice	4 shiso leaves
¾ cup water	(and extra for garnish)

Blend all ingredients except shiso until smooth then strain. Pour 1 oz into a 10oz glass over ice and top with sparkling water. Garnish with shiso leaf. Your liver will thank you.

PH TONIC

MAKES 8 PORTIONS

6 oz apple cider vinegar	2 tsp chlorophyll
3 oz lemon juice	1 quart of water
5 oz honey water	
(equal parts honey and	
warm water mixed)	

Mix all ingredients and serve straight in a glass with a couple of ice cubes. Get balanced.

GUAVA-TAHINI COLADA

SERVES 2

1 ½ cups guava juice	1 tsp coconut sugar
½ cup water	¼ tsp sumac
2 tbsp tahini	1 pinch Aleppo

Blend all ingredients except Aleppo and pour over ice. Garnish with a pinch of Aleppo. Grab some rays and elevate those legs.

FLOURLESS CHOCOLATE CAKE
WITH CARAMELIZED BANANA CREAM:

THE ANSWER TO EVERYTHING, DON'T FIGHT IT

MAKES 1 CAKE OR 6-8 INDIVIDUAL CAKES

CAKE

12 oz dark chocolate
2 sticks butter,
   cut into pieces

5 large eggs, room
   temperature
1 ¼ cups of sugar

In a double boiler, melt the chocolate and butter stirring until combined. Remove from heat and set aside.

In another bowl, mix the eggs and sugar until pale yellow and fluffy. Add the egg mixture to the chocolate, very slowly, a tiny bit at a time. If you add it all at once, you'll have scrambled eggs.

Pour batter into an 8-inch cake pan, or individual ramekins.

Make a water bath:

Cover the cake pan with foil and place into a larger roasting pan. Fill roasting pan with cold water until it's about halfway up the side of the cake pan.

Transfer the roasting pan to the oven and bake at 350 °F for 75 minutes.

Cake is done when toothpick inserted in the middle comes out clean. Remove from water bath, remove foil, and let cool completely.

CREAM

2 bananas, cut
   into pieces
½ cup brown sugar,
   divided

2 tbsp butter
1 ½ cups heavy cream
1 tsp cinnamon
1 tsp vanilla extract

While cake is baking, make your banana cream:

Melt butter in a non-stick pan. Stir in ¼ cup brown sugar until melted. Add bananas and caramelize. Transfer them to a bowl and stir and mash with a wooden spoon until a creamy purée is formed. Let cool.

In another bowl, whisk cream with the remaining ¼ cup of brown sugar, cinnamon, and vanilla until it's firm. Add the banana puree and keep mixing until it's fully incorporated and begins to set.

Serve cake topped with banana cream to taste. We garnish ours with toasted buckwheat and banana chips. Sub any nut, coconut flakes, or whatever floats your boat.

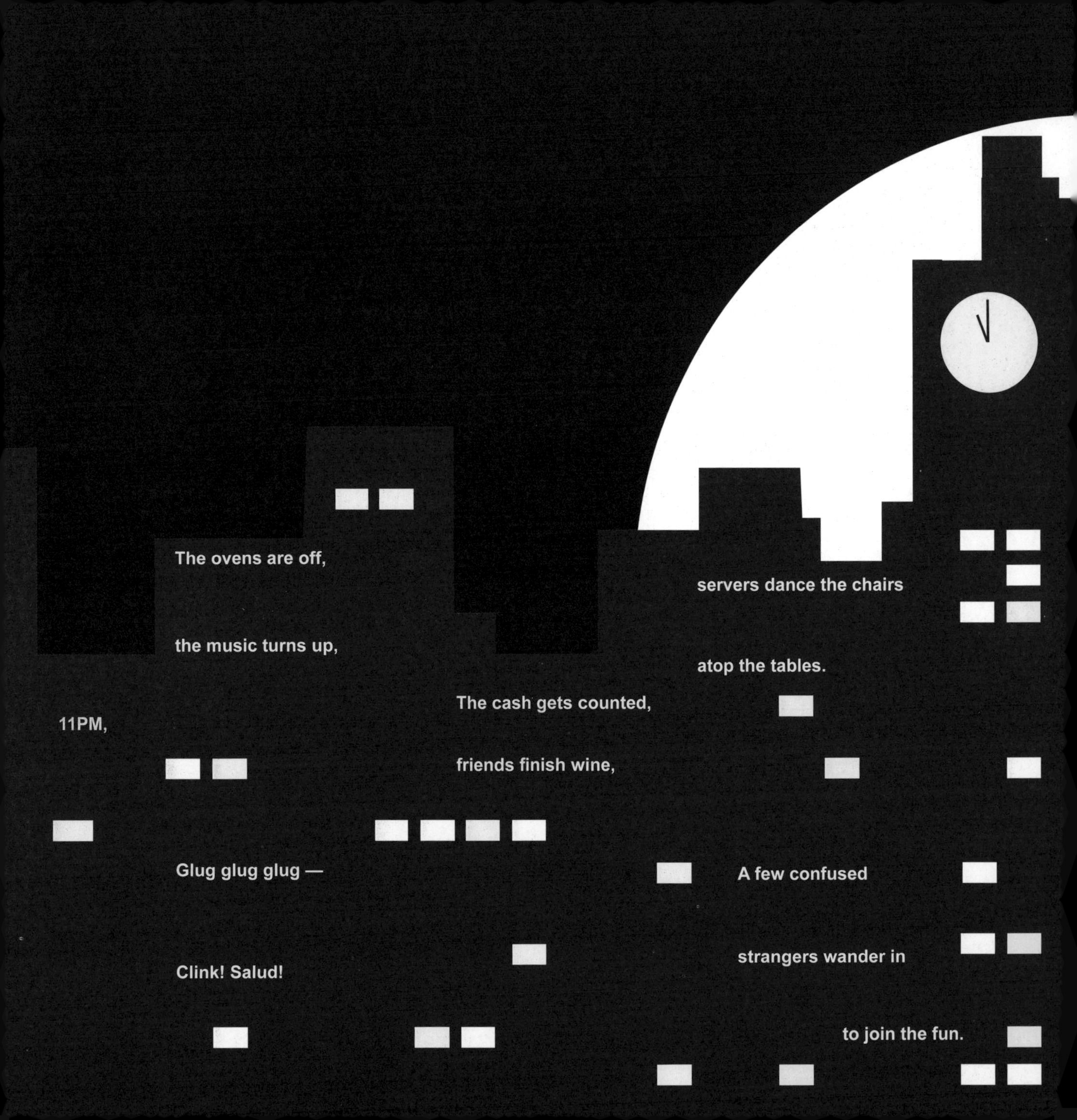

The ovens are off,

the music turns up,

11PM,

Glug glug glug —

Clink! Salud!

The cash gets counted,

friends finish wine,

servers dance the chairs

atop the tables.

A few confused

strangers wander in

to join the fun.

11:00PM

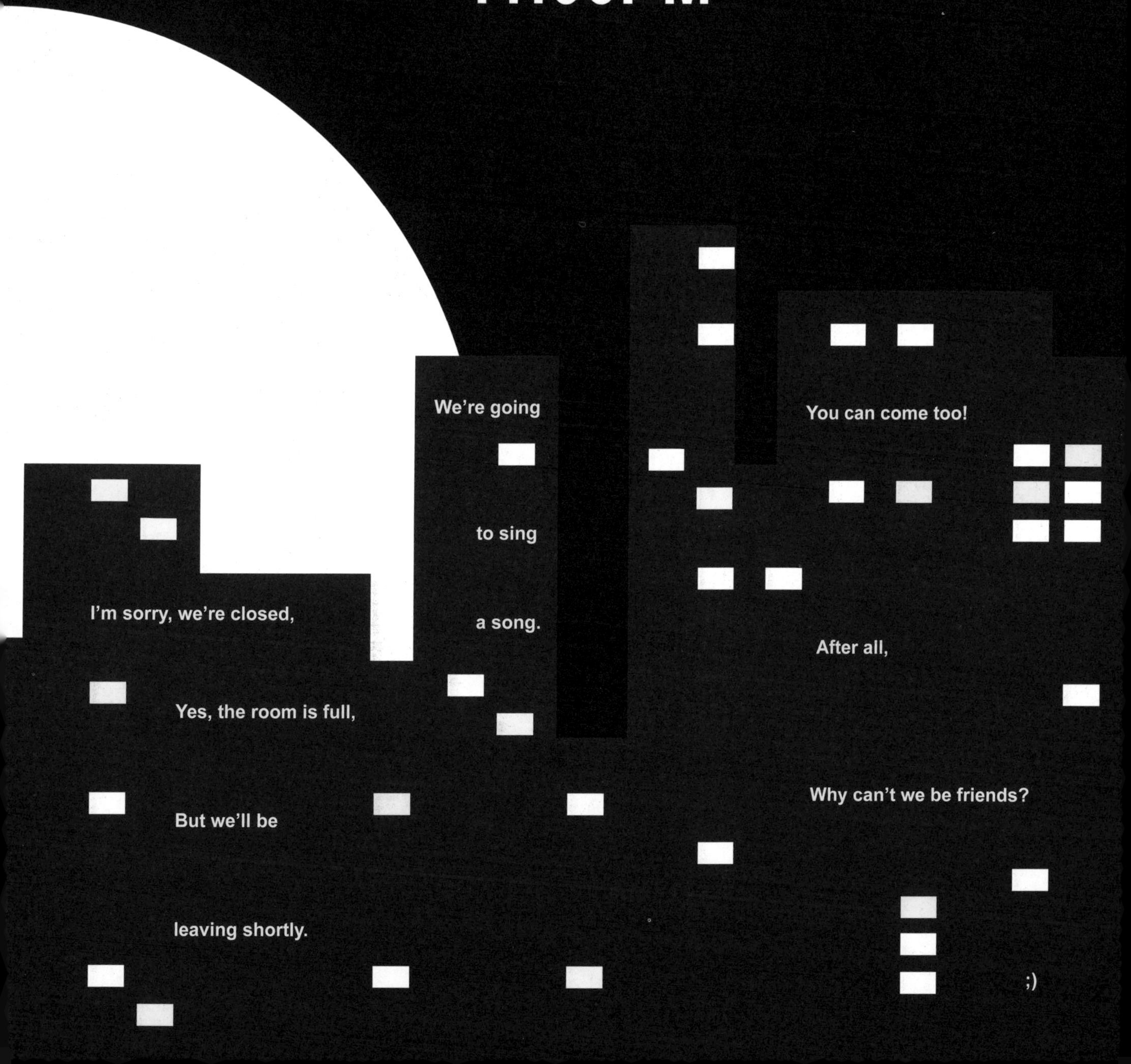

We're going

to sing

a song.

You can come too!

I'm sorry, we're closed,

Yes, the room is full,

After all,

But we'll be

Why can't we be friends?

leaving shortly.

;)

ADELE
"Mr. Cellophane"
from Chicago

AERIAL
"Love on the Brain"
Rihanna

ALBERTO
"Amiga"
Roberto Carlos

ALISSA
"Two Princes"
Spin Doctors

ALLEGRA
"Lovefool"
The Cardigans

ANDREI
"Baby"
Gal Costa

BRECKYN
"This Magic Moment"
The Drifters

CHEYNNA
"Believe"
Cher

CYNTHIA
"Picture"
Kid Rock and Sheryl Crow

DAN
"Tougher Than The Rest"
Bruce Springsteen

DENNIS
"Mia"
Bad Bunny feat. Drake

DIEGO
"Tres Semanas"
Marco Antonio Solis

DONOVAN
"So Into You"
Tamia

ERIN
"What's Up?"
4 Non Blondes

EVAN
Anything in the key of D at
around 90-100 BPM

FREDDY
"Motivos"
Vicente Fernández

GEDELIN
"Mi"
Natalia Jiménez

GIULIO
"Never Gonna Give You Up"
Rick Astley

GLEN
"Need You Tonight"
INXS

HANNAH
"Wuthering Heights"
Kate Bush

ISRAEL
"Vivir Mi Vida"
Tempo feat. Farruko

JAIR
"¿Y Cómo es Él?"
Jovanny Cadena

JAMES
"Lyin' Eyes"
The Eagles

JOHNNY
"Let Me Love You"
Mario

JOSH
"U Got It Bad"
Usher

JULIO
"Julio Perez Leon"
Los Tigres del Norte

JUSTINE
"I'm The Only One"
Melissa Etheridge

KELLIAN
"What A Wonderful World"
Louis Armstrong

KRYSTEN
"Iris"
Goo Goo Dolls

LEO
"Amiga"
Roberto Carlos

LIAM
"Eyes Without a Face"
Billy Idol

MARY
"Rocky Raccoon"
The Beatles

MEETKA
"It's Oh So Quiet"
Bjork

RAFA
"Un Dia A La Vaz"
Los Tigres del Norte

REID
"Como la Flor"
Selena

REWA
"Shadowboxer"
Fiona Apple

RUBY
"Walk on By"
Dionne Warwick

SABRINA
"Red Red Wine"
UB40

SAMMI
"Total Eclipse of the Heart"
Bonnie Tyler

SARA
"Jane Says"
Jane's Addiction

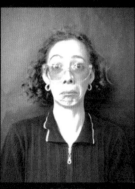

SOPHIE
"Pure Shores"
All Saints

SYLVIE
"Something to Talk About"
Bonnie Raitt

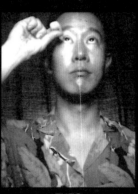

THEO
"Islands in the Stream"
Dolly Parton + Kenny Rogers

TONIANN
"Diamonds and Pearls"
Prince

VALENTE
"Low Rider"
War

WALFRED
"Tu Forma De Ser"
Alberto y Roberto

YEUNG
"Forever Young"
Rod Stewart

YOMA
"Crowds"
Bauhaus

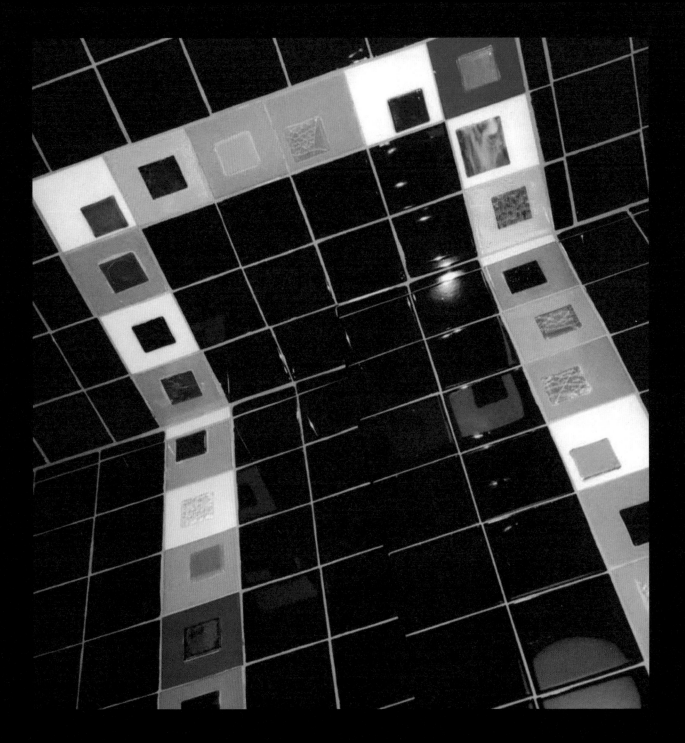

Sabrina sends thanks and love to Glen, baby Lucky, her Mom and Carol.

Alissa sends hugs and kisses to her Mom + Dad, Mame, Beth, Suzanne, Aurelia, Graham, and sweet peas Henry + Rowan.

We would like to thank Sophie, our invaluable third witch and forever partner in crime; Alberto and Diego and their team for running the show while feeding the entire neighborhood in a single day, every day; our entire Dimes family, without whom we would be lost at sea, and "Forever" Yeung for keeping our bench warm.

Special additional thanks to everyone who helped bring this project to life especially Serena Chen, Whitney Mallett, Zola Phillips, Immanuel Yang and to Cynthia Leung for the initial spark, vision and support.

Published by
Karma Books, New York

Photography: Mary Manning

Text: Alissa Wagner and Toniann Fernandez

Design: Erin Knutson

Creative Direction: Sabrina De Sousa

Introduction by Cynthia Leung

Photography on pages 8-19, 48-64 by Yudi Ela

Yearbook portraits were taken with love by the subjects at photobooths around the city.

ISBN 978-1-949172-36-2

Publication © 2019 Dimes

Love Toast Recipe by Stevie Dance, p 31
Bulgur recipe inspired by Chermoula Eggplant with Bulgur and Yogurt
    from "Jerusalem" by Sami Tamimi and Yotam Ottolenghi, p 78
Cilantro Salsa Verde by Zola Phillips, p 91
Cornbread recipe adapted from "The Angelica Home Kitchen"
    by Leslie McEachern, p 104
Pozole Recipe by Alberto Herrera, p 107
Vegan Mac and Cheese adapted from recipe by Zola Phillips, p 110
Flowers by Metaflora, p 121
Wheatgrass Margarita recipe by Arley Marks, p 131
Chocolate Cake recipe by Antonella Tignanelli, p 135